THE GOLDEN AGE
OF THE
STEAM LOCOMOTIVE

With Over 250 Classic Illustrations

J. G. Pangborn

Dover Publications, Inc.
Mineola, New York

Bibliographical Note

This Dover edition, first published in 2003, is an unabridged republication of the work originally published in 1894 by Winchell Printing Company, New York, under the title *The World's Rail Way: Historical, Descriptive, Illustrative.* The color plates from the original edition are reproduced here in black and white.

Library of Congress Cataloging-in-Publication Data

Pangborn, J. G. (Joseph Gladding), 1844–1914.
    The golden age of the steam locomotive : with over 250 classic illustrations / J.G. Pangborn.
       p. cm.
    Reprint. Originally published: New York : Winchell Printing Co., 1894.
    ISBN 0-486-42824-9 (pbk.)
    1. Steam locomotives—History. I. Title.

TJ603 .P33 2003
625.26'1—dc21

2002035006

Manufactured in the United States of America
Dover Publications, Inc., 31 East 2nd Street, Mineola, N.Y. 11501

· TO · MARSHALL · FIELD : WHOSE · CONCEPTION · OF · THE ·
· STEWARDSHIP · OF · THE · MILLIONS · WITH · WHICH · HE ·
· HAS   BEEN · BLESSED : LED · TO · THEIR · EMPLOYMENT ·
· FOR · THE · EDUCATION · AND · ELEVATION · OF · HIS ·
· FELLOW · MAN · THROUGH · THE · COLUMBIAN · MUSEUM :
· A · COMPONENT · PART · OF · WHICH · INSTITUTION · IS ·
· THE · PIONEER · MUSEUM · OF · THE · WORLD'S · RAIL ·
· WAY : THIS · VOLUME · IS · APPRECIATIVELY · DEDICATED ·

THE preparation of this volume has not been independent of preceding works upon the rail way, although they are not indicated in the text. The subject is so vast in its ramifications, so important in its details, that to devote space to reference to authorities is to sacrifice in other directions. To mention few would be an invidious distinction, while to draw the best from all and combine with that which has not hitherto been given the world is regarded in this instance as the service the rail way public at large will best appreciate.

Much the greater portion of the work is devoted to the earlier periods of evolution and progress, in the belief that such is the more instructive and of the larger value in enabling comprehension of the steps which have led up to the development of to-day.

With the latter the present generation is more or less familiar, and appreciating this, the fact that the illustrations include examples to the period of the Columbian Exposition will be recognized as affording opportunity for comparison pictorially, but not at the expense in the text of a curtailment of historical detail.

The effort has been to narrate rather than to exploit, and to tell the story plainly and simply, without thought of literary embellishment, and entirely devoid of bias in favor of any one. The facts are given as the chronology is maintained, and from them conclusions may be drawn as the reader believes justified.

THE WORLD'S RAIL WAY

Single Wooden Rail 1676

SIR Isaac Newton, fresh from his comparatively recent discussion with Hooke on the subject of universal gravitation, and now engrossed in the latest measurement of a degree of the meridian by the French astronomer, Picard, nevertheless has time, in 1680, to give at the least a passing thought in still another channel, so wide, varied and deep is the mind of the philosopher.

The links in the history of steam are woven from Hero to Huyghens. Papin, the young Frenchman, is in London, so too Moreland and Savary, and all are solving, or attempting to solve, the problems of steam. Newton's conception of force is that of Hero's, but the idea of making it serve as a means of propulsion is his own. He is the first to have a thought in this direction. Speaking of the quantities of elastic vapors produced by the action of fire, he says, after describing the filling of a ball with water, and the consequent change to vapor by the heat :

"We have a more sensible effect of the elasticity of vapors if the hole be made bigger and stopped, and then the ball be laid upon the fire till the water boils violently ; after this, if the ball be set upon little wheels, so as to

9

The Newton 1680

Double Wooden Rail 1700

move easily upon a horizontal plane, and the hole be opened, the vapors will rush out violently one way, and the wheels and the ball at the same time will be carried the contrary way."

Newton at the time does not construct—he merely suggests; but in this he accomplishes more than the Marquis of Worcester, for the philosopher tells how the propulsion can be secured, the other simply referring to his ideas as possibilities.

For a half century, or since 1630, a form of railway has been known, Master 1630 Beaumont as early as the period mentioned having expended some thirty thousand pounds in perfecting a substitute for common roads from his coal pits, near Newcastle, to the river side. Of this road Newton may have no actual knowledge, though if he has read Gray's "Chorographia," published in 1649, 1649 he has ascertained that Beaumont "within a few years consumed all his money and rode home upon his light horse." However this may be, coals are being conveyed from the mines near Newcastle to the banks of the river—on rails of timber laid exactly straight and parallel—in bulky carts, with four rollers fitting the rails, one horse thus drawing four or five chaldrons of coal. Another rail of wood is placed upon that already laid, and what is known as the "single way" becomes the "double way." The next step is to place a ledge upon the side of the rail to prevent the wagons from going out of their tracks. Papin, in 1681, invents the safety valve. Moreland, in 1683, presents what he calls 1681 his new force of fire to his Queen. Papin, in 1695, perfects his new engine 1683 for producing a vacuum by the condensation of steam, three years later Savary 1695 follows upon similar principle, while Newcomen, in 1707, 1707 produces his atmospheric engine, embracing a cylinder containing a piston driven upward by steam from a boiler, and forced downward by atmospheric pressure, when the steam below the piston is removed by condensation.

In 1713 the lad Potter 1713 through a characteristic, boyish evasion of work, makes the valve gear automatic by leading cords to the beam, and in 1718 Beighton 1718 substitutes the plug rod, and

Holland Sail Chariot 1765

Common Plate Rail 1767

The Cugnot 1769

10

thus establishes the improvement upon a substantial basis. Leupold comes to

1720 the front in 1720 with his high-pressure engine having two single-acting cylinders placed upon the boiler, each with a steam pipe piston moved alternately by steam admitted through a four-way cock.

Meantime, the wear and tear upon the wooden rail ways is becoming such as to render it imperative that something be done, or else recourse must be had

1737 to the common roads again. At Whitehaven, in 1737, the plan is introduced of placing cast-iron plates upon the face of the wooden rails, which, owing to

1750 the heavy wagons still used, causes interminable breakage. In 1750 cast-iron wheels are in vogue, but used only on the forward axle, the wooden wheels being retained on the rear axle under the belief that the brake will hold only on the old style wheels. Later experiments lead to such extension of the brake lever as to bring about the substitution of iron wheels on all axles, which change also results in a reduction of the weight upon the rails, through the use of lighter wagons and linking them together, thus enabling the transport of more coal at one time than is possible by means of the heavy wagons. As the years go by the natural course of events leads to the adoption of the iron, or plate, rail instead of the more or less irregular plates upon the wooden

1767 rail. The first are made at the Colebrook Iron Works in 1767. They are about five feet in length, four inches in breadth and an inch and a quarter thick, each rail having three holes to fasten it to the wood below. The flange is cast upon the rail, the periphery of the wheel being made quite flat and narrow.

While this is going on as regards the rail way, the various inventors adapters and investigators of steam and its possibilities are pursuing the tenor of their minds through discussion, claims and counterclaims, no marked advance in actual progress being achieved until Watt appears upon the scene. Combative, confident, and not over chary of the feelings or opinions of others who have preceded him, there soon is an activity that bodes much in circles which have been somewhat sluggish. However, Watt no more leans to a recognition of the chances of other use of steam power than pumping out mines and similar fields of operation, than do the pioneers in steam engine development or his immediate cotemporaries. To be sure, his friend, Dr. Robinson, has been importuning him for some time to apply steam power to

11

the moving of wheel carriages, and even prior to the good doctor's suggestions he has known of that other good doctor, Darwin's, entreaties to his (Watt's) partner Boulton, to construct a steam carriage, or, as he enthusiastically puts it, a "fiery chariot." But Watt, in 1769, is completely wrapped up in his plans, as set forth in the patent he has taken out, and which has to do largely with his first rotary engine.

There comes from a wholly unexpected source—not from the ranks of the scientists, as the developers of the steam engine may in this connection be termed, but from the French Army—the first propulsion by steam on land in the world. Nicholas Joseph Cugnot is a native of Void, in Lorraine, and forty years of age. He has served in both the French and the German armies, in the latter as an engineer, and published several works on military science. His knowledge of steam has been obtained more by reading than from actual experience with its properties. The conception of its possibilities comes from the thought of its adaptability for use in the propulsion of artillery, it occurring to him that with such an agency quick movement in the field can be secured better than with animal power. Considering the fact that it is something the like of which the world has never seen and scarcely anticipated, his machine, while naturally defective in more respects than one, is still remarkable. In it is the first application of the high-pressure, or non-condensing, engine, with cylinders and pistons, to the production of rotary motion, and it is mounted on three wheels, the rear pair being merely carriers, while the front wheel is the driving, as well as the guiding, wheel. There are two vertical, single-acting cylinders, placed astride the forward, or guiding, wheel, a little in advance of the vertical center, with which they move from side to side as the engine is turned. The steam is admitted above the pistons only, and exhausted from the lower, or open, end of the cylinder. The cylinders are each connected to one end of a beam, fulcrumed to its center, above the wheel, and to the same end an attachment is made to a pawl engaging a toothed wheel fixed upon the axle of the driving wheel. When steam is admitted to one of the cylinders it carries down its end of the connecting lever, the pawl engages in the rack and moves the wheel a half revolution, while the opposite end of the lever returns the other piston to its position for the work of the opposite half of the stroke. The cylinders alter-

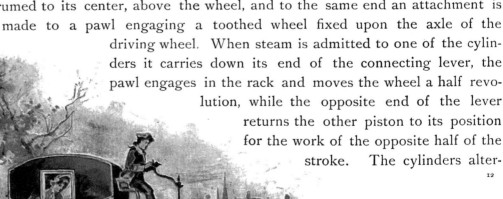

Symington
1786

nating in duty, thus propel the machine. The boiler is very much like a large copper kettle, and is attached to and swung with the guiding and driving wheel, which is operated by a rack and pinion on a perpendicular shaft, reaching up to the seat of the engineer, where a hand wheel is provided within easy reach. The trial does not, unfortunately, result in the success hoped for, the boiler being sufficient for only twelve to fifteen minutes' work, while the power produces a speed of scarcely two and a half miles an hour. One day, passing through a street in Paris, control is lost and over goes the machine, with a noise so unusual that it is regarded as a dangerous thing to further trifle with, and is locked up. Cugnot is, however, given the cross of the Legion of Honor and a pension.

Oliver Evans, in the United States, is heard from in 1779 through his per-
1779 fection of the high-pressure non-condensing steam engine, and the following year he introduces it in a stationary engine. The boiler is multitubular, and of the water tube type; the water being in the tubes, and the products of combustion passing between them. "To Oliver Evans," says Dr. Ernest Alban, the German engineer, in commenting upon this high-pressure non-condensing engine, "was it reserved to show the true value of a long-known principle, and to establish thereon a new and more simple method of applying steam, a method which will remain an eternal memorial to its introducer."

Meanwhile, in England, James Watt has grown to be almost supreme among those devoting brain power and time to the perfection of the steam engine—a supremacy even greater than his commanding genius justifies, his influence, his powerful friends, and his arrogance of supreme right literally forcing his cotemporaries to march behind him. Some of them are very close to him, notably so William Murdoch, who, lacking in personal assumption, is by no means deficient in genius. By nature timid, he is the more so when brought into immediate association with a man of Watt's strong and aggressive personality. He has an idea of the possibilities of steam for propulsion on land, and in
1784 1784 surreptitiously, so to speak, proceeds to put it into form, first in a very small working model, then half size, if not, indeed, three-quarters. Having something like an adequate realization of the necessities, he employs high-pressure steam, and this adds to his secretiveness from Watt,

13

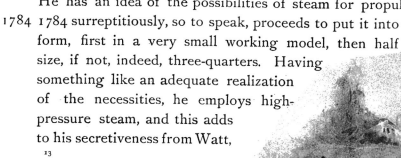

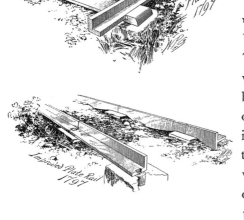

Plate Rail
1797

Improved Plate Rail
1797

who is the most bitter and persistent opponent of high pressure in all the kingdom.
Watt himself, for some reason or other, takes out a patent for a steam carriage.
The boiler, he specifies, is to be made of wooden staves joined together and fastened
with iron hoops, like a cask. The furnace is to be of iron, and placed inside of the
boiler, so as to be surrounded on every side by water. This boiler is to be placed
on a carriage the wheels of which are to receive their motion from a piston working
in a cylinder, the reciprocating motion being converted into a rotary one by
toothed wheels, revolving with a sun and planet motion, and producing the required
velocity by a common series of wheels and pinions. By means of two systems
of wheel work, differing in their proportion, he proposes to adapt the power of
the machine to the varied resistance it may have to overcome from the state of
the road. Hardly has he secured this patent than he declares : " I have relin-
quished the idea of constructing an engine on this principle owing to the danger
of bursting the boiler, and also that a great part of the power of the steam would
be lost because no vacuum would be formed to assist the descent of the piston."
Watt goes no further in this direction, except as an obstructionist. He complains
that Murdoch, who is his assistant at the Soho factory, gives too much of his
time to the study of the possibilities of the steam carriage ; the latter hurries on
with his invention and makes his trials of it at night, very much to the alarm of
the venerable Vicar of Redruth, whose quiet and peaceful
walk in a lonely lane leading to his church, one serene
evening, is suddenly broken in upon by what to his horror
appears as an indescribable creature of legs, arms and
wheels, whose body seems glowing with internal fire, and
whose rapid gasps for breath indicate a fierce struggle for
existence. The reverend man's cries for help speedily bring
Murdoch to the scene, with the assuring explanation that
the terrible apparition is not an incarnation or a messenger
from the Evil One, but only a runaway engine.

The engine is carried on three wheels, one of the rear
pair being keyed to the axle, which is driven by a single
crank. To this crank is attached the lower end of a connecting rod, the upper end being fastened to a horizontal
beam. The forward end of this beam is pivoted to a post
extending up from the platform, where the
engineer stands. To the other end of

14

Trevithick's
1800

the beam is attached the piston rod, and between the ends, rather nearer the cylinder end, is the connecting rod attachment, the beam being forked from the connecting rod attachment to the cylinder end. The single steam cylinder extends a short distance into the top of the square copper boiler, which is secured to the engineer's platform, and heated by a lamp suspended underneath it. The cylinder is double-acting, and the valves controlling the admission of steam are placed within a pipe chamber attached to the front of the cylinder. A stem from the valve passes upward between the jaws of the beam fork and carries two adjustable sleeves, one above and one below the lever. As the lever moves up and down it comes in contact with these sleeves and moves the valves for the admission of steam. The exhaust is through the piston rod, which is hollow and has slotted openings at its upper end opening to the atmosphere. The front wheel is pivoted on an upright shaft extending through the platform, with a handle affixed thereto, furnishing a means by which the engineer can direct the course of the machine. Such is the first propulsion by steam on English soil in history, and it is accomplished through the same form of engine as that devised in the United States by Oliver Evans five years previously, in his high-pressure, non-condensing engine of the "grasshopper" type. The speed attained by the Murdoch is from six to eight miles an hour, but its control is uncertain, owing to the gear being all on one side. Further experiments by the inventor must be at the expense of his losing his place with Watt, and for various reasons not wishing this to occur, Murdoch steps to the rear and others come to the front.

Back in New England, in the land of the free and the brave, and that sort of 1785 thing, Nathan Read, of Salem, Massachusetts, is, in 1785, experimenting with small tubes, sometimes of brass and other times of copper, for use in steam boilers, his primary idea being to secure rapid transmission of the heat to the water, thus permitting the use of a smaller area of heating surface and of a smaller boiler.

Like Cugnot's and Murdoch's, the steam car-   riage of William 1786 Symington's conception in 1786 takes form on   three wheels, one the guiding and the other two carrying the engine and boiler, the motion being communicated from the engine to the wheels by a ratchet. In this engine, for the first time, provision for passengers is looked to, and a coach body suspended between the wheels

15

gives the affair quite a shapely appearance. His engine is on the low-pressure, or condensing, principle, with a single cylinder, but beyond the completion of the model Symington does not go.

Oliver Evans' application to the Legislature of Pennsylvania in 1786 for permission to introduce his steam engine in steam carriages is refused ; but the succeeding year he secures a patent on his high-pressure engine, and erects one in Philadelphia. He is more fortunate in Maryland : that State grants him the right to use his steam wagons, and, full of enthusiasm, he predicts that "the time will come when carriages propelled by steam will be in general use for the transportation of passengers as well as goods, and will travel at the rate of fifteen miles an hour, or three hundred miles a day." Evans at this time, however, carries his plans no further in the direction of his wagons or carriages than the securing of the grant.

With 1789 there comes an organic change in the rail way in the substitution, 1789 brought about by Jessop's edge rail, of the flanged wheel for the flanged rail. This rail consists of a bar of cast iron from three to four feet long, with a web about one-half or three-quarters of an inch thick, swelling out at the head to two or two and a half inches in width. The rails have a flat base for a short distance at each end, through which square holes are cast for the pins or nails to pass through for fastening them to the sleepers. The wheel run upon these rails has a cylindrical rim, with the projection at one side, called the "flanch," to keep it in place there being a square hole through the nave for the axle. The wheel is cast in one piece, with spokes about half an inch thick and four inches broad, the rim one inch thick and the flanch one inch deep.

In the succeeding year the first move in the direction of a steam car- 1790 riage, or wagon, is made in America, Nathan Read taking out a patent and following it with the completion of a model. It has four wheels, the front pair being pivoted at the center and controlled by a horizontal sheave and rope, The sheave is located well back near the boiler, and operated in guiding the machine by a hand wheel placed above the platform, in a suitable position to be convenient for the engineer. The boiler is square and overhanging at the back end ; it is multitubular, being Read's first perfection of his system of copper or brass tubes, and the initial introduction of this class of boiler. The driving pair of wheels are placed forward of the square boiler and

16

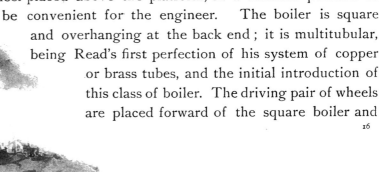

just in front of these wheels are two horizontal cylinders, one on each side of the engine. Piston rods from the cylinders reach backward, and the connection to the wheel is very novel and ingenious. The inside hub of each wheel has ratchet teeth formed on it for one-half its diameter ; into these teeth work corresponding ones on horizontal racks, one above the hub and one below. When the piston moves toward the back end of the cylinder the upper rack engages the hub teeth and revolves the wheels forward, and when the return stroke is made the lower rack engages the hub teeth and continues the revolution. Steam pipes enter each cylinder head, front and back, near the inside and exhaust pipes on the opposite or outside of the heads. There are two steam valves and two exhaust valves to each cylinder, operated by an attachment to the racks, the exhaust being into the atmosphere. Each cylinder has its steam pipe from the boiler provided with a stop cock, and one cylinder or both can be worked at the same time. This is the pioneer conception of the propulsion by steam on land in America, and Read, soon finding it anything but encouraging to secure the necessary funds for construction, stops at the model and turns his attention to other inventions, of which he is remarkably prolific.

Chairs for rails appear in 1792 ; the mode practiced in fastening them to the 1792 blocks is to cast a circular hole on each side of the base of the chair and a hole of similar size is drilled into the block. An oak plug is then driven through both, which, having a wedge-shaped head, and being dry when driven, secures the chair to the sleeper. The chairs have a flat base four by seven inches, and three-quarters of an inch thick, the upper surface upon which the rail rests being also flat and horizontal. Two bosses are cast on the base, with a distance between them equal to the thickness of the web, forming a pocket into which the ends of the rails are inserted. The pins that are driven through the holes into the chairs and rails fasten the ends of the rails to the bosses of the chairs, and prevent their ends from starting upward out of the recess, and the sides, or cheeks, of the bosses prevent the ends of the rail from moving laterally. Stone supports, one foot or thereabouts square and eight inches deep, or square pieces of timber firmly embedded in the surface of the road, form the sleepers on which the chairs rest when in position.

Evans within the next two years completes, for forwarding to England, the special

17.

Concave Rail, Wales, 1803

Trevithick's 1803

drawings and specifications of his steam engines and in the Fall of 1794 they 1794 are taken across the Atlantic by Mr. Joseph Stacy Sampson for the inspection of English engineers and others engaged in developing steam into an agency of widespread usefulness. James Watt at this time is in the zenith of his power and influence, holding practically a monopoly of the construction of the steam engine in Europe, and very sharply guarding every attempt to accomplish anything without the use of his patents and the consequent payment of tribute.

There is near him in Cornwall one who has vainly endeavored to evade the Watt patents and accomplish something. Richard Trevithick is the man, and a stalwart son of toil he is. Large and powerful to a degree, which has made him the Samson of his locality; sturdy and persevering, with a genius for practice in strong contrast to that of several of his cotemporaries for theory, Trevithick is determined to get his ideas into shape for demonstration if increasing application and study will accomplish it. Late in 1796 he has a small model of 1796 a steam wagon or carriage in motion at his house in Camborne, and by the year 1800, when Watt's patent expires, and Trevithick is thus released from the bonds 1800 that held him, he has his model of a high-pressure steam engine with cylindrical boiler adapted to use for propulsion on common roads completed, and running around his room. This machine is on three wheels, one forward and pivoted to use for guiding. The boiler is horizontal, with a chamber at the front end in which to insert a heated bar of iron for generating steam. There is one double-acting cylinder, vertical, and extending a short distance into the boiler. The piston rod extends through the top of the cylinder to a cross-head above, carried on two round guides. The cross-head is long enough to reach from side to side of the engine, and has attached to each end a connecting rod, which extends to the back, or driving, wheels. Attached to the left-hand wheel is a spur gear which gears with a pinion on the shaft of an unusually large fly-wheel. The admission and exhaust valve is a four-way plug cock located in a chamber at the back of the cylinder. The cock has a handle which is passed through a slot in a vertical rod attached to the cross-head at the upper end and running through a guide at its lower end. As the cross-head moves it carries the rod with it, and the ends of the slot coming in contact with the handle of the plug valve turn it so as to admit and exhaust steam alternately to each end of the cylinder. The exhaust is direct into the atmosphere. Under the front axle at each side, inside of the wheel, are jack screws to raise the machine off its wheels and make it a stationary engine. The idea is here, if not its full

₁₈

realization, and it is sufficient to encourage and lead to other experiments. The locomotive is conceived. As if in common, the rail way the same year advances, Benjamin Outram introducing stone props, or sleepers, instead of timber, for supporting the ends or joinings of the rails, thus insuring greater strength to support heavy loads. Trevithick, it now being late in the year 1800, determines to construct a steam engine of full size and of such capacity as will enable actual operation upon the roads in his vicinity. His tools and facilities are those of a country blacksmith, and therefore progress is exceedingly slow, and

1801 it is not until Christmas time of 1801 that Captain Dick's " Puffer," as the people call it, is on the road puffing and blowing after a manner simply astonishing to the natives. Getting some of them aboard, the first transportation of passengers by the force of steam in the world is recorded, and the " Puffer" moves off at the rate of four or five miles an hour. The preliminary trial is more than satisfactory, particularly in the ability demonstrated to ascend grades. The great difficulty is in keeping up the steam pressure, which it is attempted to accomplish by the use of cylindrical or horizontal bellows worked by the engine itself. The engine is upon four wheels, the boiler of the horizontal return flue type, known as the " Lancashire," and of Oliver Evans' devising, that is to say, the same as his built and used in America. There is one vertical cylinder in this Trevithick of 1801, and it is located in the top of the boiler. The piston rod extends through the upper cylinder head to the cross-head, and the connecting rod down to the back wheels. The two front wheels are arranged in a truck, and the exhaust is into the stack. There is a pump with feed water heater, and a blower on top of the boiler with a pipe to an ash pit. The turning of the exhaust steam into the stack is to get rid of the noise, and thus not only to a certain extent calm the apprehension of the people, but at the same time enable the driving of horses within something like a reasonable distance of the machine when it is under full head of steam. Trouble being found with adhesion, Trevithick proposes to obviate it by, to quote his own words, " making the external periphery of the wheels uneven by projecting heads of nails or bolts, or cross grooves or fittings to rail roads when required, and that in cases of a hard pull we will cause a lever, bolt or claw to project through the rim of one or both the wheels so as to take hold of the ground." Trevithick

TREVITHICK'S BURIAL PLACE IN POTTER'S FIELD

Llannelly Rail Wales 1808

having determined that propulsion on land was not only feasible, but wholly practical, proceeds to design and construct a steam carriage which is an improvement upon the "Puffer," it being a steam stage coach, in fact, with all the comforts of the coach as to passenger accommodations and the propelling power so compact and efficient as to render horses no longer necessary. The boiler is cylindrical and of wrought iron, with two internal tubes for firebox and flue. The cylinder is fixed in the boiler and placed in a horizontal position close behind the driving axle. Changeable tooth wheels with couplings connect the crank axle with the driving wheels. A fly-wheel equalizes the movement and serves as a means for applying a brake. The four-way cock is worked by spring levers resting against projections on the crank shaft, and is an eccentric simplified. A spring lever also works the feed pump. The two driving wheels are of wood, ten feet in diameter, the two guide wheels being four feet in diameter. Although Trevithick has his carriage in actual operation, and has done many new things in the way of adapting, applying and inventing machinery to meet requirements, his path is anything but one of roses. Watt, who is still bitter and deep-rooted in his prejudice against high pressure, declares that Trevithick ought to be hanged for persisting in employing it in his inventions, and there are not a few others who echo these sentiments, for Watt is great and powerful, and poor Trevithick is neither, so far as public estimation goes. The bad roads are also a source of trouble to Trevithick, who finds that they operate sadly against the efficiency of his steam carriage. With Vivian, his cousin, friend and backer, he takes the invention to London, and there it is practically lost sight of, the adherents of Watt and the low-pressure steam vacuum engine strongly condemning it, and declaring that Trevithick, in the high-pressure engine without condenser, degraded the principle because it did not use condensing water.

Trevithick's adherents are few and far between; still, there are enough of them to keep up a discussion of the relative merits of high and low pressure, the possibilities of transport on land by steam, and kindred topics. The outcome is finally a wager, in which Trevithick undertakes to design and build a locomotive, which upon being placed on the Merthyr Tydvil tram or railway in South Wales shall, with its own power, propel wagons containing ten tons of iron. The sum bet is five hundred guineas, and Trevithick, positive that he will win them, builds at Penydarran, in 1803, the first locomotive in the

1803

20

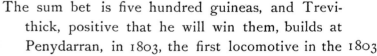

Trevithick's 1808

1803 world.   The tramway at Merthyr Tydvil has one foot elevation in fifty, and is very far from being adapted to the moving of a locomotive.   There are three or four little cars on the tramway, each with four wheels, and the arrangement for hauling them together, and thus enable the transportation of rails of several feet in length, is such as to admit of passing around curves and obviating difficulty in this respect where the line is other than straight.   Two or more cars are coupled by an iron rod, which has a hook at each end and which fits into rings or eye-bolts on the cars.   The iron rests upon elongated U-shaped supports which are pivoted down through the center of the car and swing one way or the other as necessity requires.   To five of these little cars, upon which are loaded ten tons of iron, which in turn afford a resting place for no less than seventy people attracted to the scene by its novelty, Trevithick attaches his locomotive, and the first movement by steam upon rails in the world is an accomplished fact. Progress is slow, for trees have to be cut down here and large rocks removed there, no thought of a locomotive ever having entered the heads of those who built the road.   When moving the speed averaged is at the rate of nearly five miles an hour, but so many are the difficulties encountered in getting unobstructed passage over the route that it requires four hours to cover the nine miles. No water is put into the boiler after the start, and the consumption of coal is two hundredweight.   Trevithick wins his bet, remains about the tramway several days, during which other trips are made, and despite broken tram-plates, sharp curves and inclines, the locomotive goes and comes, very much to the gratification of some and the chagrin of others.   It is on four flangeless wheels, three feet nine inches in diameter, placed four feet one inch from center to center, with a horizontal boiler four feet three inches in diameter by six feet in length.   There is a single cylinder eight and a quarter inches in diameter by four feet six inch stroke, fixed in the front end of the boiler   horizontally, with the

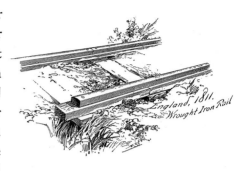

England, 1811.
Wrought Iron Rail

West
Blenkinsop's Rack Rail
1812

piston rod connected to a long cross-head which reaches across the engine far enough to connect on each side to a rod extending back by the side of the boiler to a crank on a cross shaft located at the back end.   This shaft has a large balance wheel at one end and at the opposite end a spur wheel, which gears into a larger spur wheel on the boiler centrally above the driving wheels and gearing into a spur wheel

Blenkinsop
1812

on each driving axle. Thus by means of the four gears motion is conveyed from the cranks to the driving wheels. The valve mechanism for the steam cylinder is a four-way cock worked by a rod, having two adjustable collars against which the cross-head moves in its travel back and forth, moving the cock so it will admit steam at one end of the cylinder while exhausting it at the other. A handle is provided at the outer end of the rod for the operation of the valve by hand. The boiler has an internal return flue, the fire door and stack being both located at the front end. A flange on the rails guides the wheels.

While Trevithick is accomplishing results in England, Oliver Evans, to whom the father of the locomotive is undoubtedly very largely indebted for his progress in high-pressure development, is in America demonstrating that where there is a will there is a way. As in the case of Trevithick, his trials and tribulations are many. They are both in advance of the age, Evans pre-eminently so. His mind is a mine, and the manner in which he delves into it, and what he brings forth, cannot be comprehended by his cotemporaries in his own country, above the very tallest of whom he towers head and shoulders. With no funds to mention of his own, no moneyed friends, and several persistent enemies—made such because of his refusal to desist on the lines he is operating—Evans' position in 1804 is not one productive of satisfac- 1804 tion. To add to his disappointments he learns that his single and double flue boilers have come into such use in England as to be known by local names, as, for instance, the " Cornish," the " Lancashire," etc., etc., while his high-pressure non-condensing engine has been made the foundation for most successful progress without so much as a thank you from anybody. Compelled to give most of his time to the devising and improving of flour-mill machinery in order to maintain himself, Evans, who has all along been the most earnest advocate and promoter of the possibilities of the use of steam for land propulsion, is finally led to a practical application of his proposed plans through the necessity of getting a dredging machine he has constructed for the city authorities of Philadelphia from his factory to the river, some distance away. It is a big clumsy thing, a square-

Hedley's Model 1813

1804 end scow, in fact, weighing some forty thousand pounds, and anything but an encouraging object to be the first vehicle ever propelled by steam on land in America, if not, indeed, the first actually practical propulsion by steam in the world. Evans, eager and confident that his theories of surface movement by steam are thoroughly sound, jacks up his dredging boat, puts axles and wheels under it, and then, connecting his machinery with the wheels, steams out of his shop off over the cobble stones of Market street to the Schuylkill River; there running into the water he changes the connection from the carrying wheels to the paddle-wheel astern, and sails down the Schuylkill to the Delaware and up that stream to the point where he delivers the machine, according to contract. Looking at it as it stands, the structure is not a pretty one, but it is suggestive of business. The boiler is of a comparatively small diameter, and quite long, having one straight tube from end to end. The casing or setting is in brick work so arranged as to have a fire on grates under one end, the flames passing under the boiler its whole length and returning to the smoke stack at the front end through a central tube. A vertical cylinder five inches in diameter with a nineteen inches stroke has its piston rod connected direct to an overhead wooden beam near one end, the other end being suspended by a movable link in order to allow the beam to move up and down parallel with the piston. The beam is further guided in its course by an upright post, to which it is held by a strap which slides up and down on the post as the beam moves. The beam has a second connection, which is to a crank on the fly-wheel shaft. The valves are worked by means of gear from the main shaft. A tank is provided and a pump driven from the wooden beam supplies water to the boiler. The propelling power on land is by the means of an endless rope from a groove wheel on the fly-wheel shaft to one on the road wheel shaft, and another endless rope from one groove wheel to another groove wheel. This experiment Evans finds costs him more than the profits on the dredger, and he goes back to his flour-milling machinery, convinced that it is the only path open upon which he can work out a living.

Trevithick, in England, is pegging away on a half-dozen things, among them a traveling steam crane and a fire engine for the West India Docks. Watt and his partner, Boulton, are still after him and the high-pressure steam engine on the ground that the lives of the public are endangered, and they appeal to Parliament for an Act

23

Puffing Billy 1813

Geo Stephenson

to prevent the construction of any more engines on the high-pressure principle. Meanwhile, Trevithick is testing to a further extent his first locomotive, and is greatly elated to find that it will haul twenty-five tons with ease. The next year he is ready with another and a much simpler locomotive than his first. The creation of 1805 has a boiler of cylindrical form 1805 with flat ends, the fire being contained in a single large tube at one end; the tube extends nearly to the opposite end of the boiler and then, being diminished in size, is turned and brought out at the chimney or stack. The fire tube is completely surrounded with water, by which arrangement steam is generated with great rapidity and is of a high degree of elasticity. The cylinder is vertical, located inside of the boiler and extends nearly to the bottom. A four-way cock admits the steam alternately above and below the piston, and the exhaust is into the stack. The upper end of the piston rod is attached to a cross-head, which moves up and down on vertical guides, and from the ends of this cross-head connecting rods project down to cranks fixed on the axles of the four wheels, which are thus caused to revolve like the fly-wheel of a stationary engine. The departure in general form and construction from his previous effort is marked, and Trevithick, apparently content with one or two more or less satisfactory trials, then busies himself with other plans.

Malleable iron rails are introduced on the Walbottle Colliery, near Newcastle, being one to two inches square, two feet in length and connected by a half-lap joint with one pin, one end of each rail projecting two or three inches beyond the end of that adjoining. Results are not encouraging, as the rails, being narrow, cut the wheels badly. Germany appears to be waking up to the importance of a tramway instead of a canal to connect the Moldau with the Danube, and now, in 1807, Boston has 1807 something like one on Beacon Hill, with more of an incline, however, than a tramway. A wooden way is also talked of in Philadelphia, and in 1808 the Wylam 1808 tramway, in England, is reconstructed, the wooden rails being replaced by others in the form of cast-iron plates. Trevithick again comes forward, and in his "Catch Me Who Can," of 1808, presents his highest type of locomotive. He determines that London shall

24

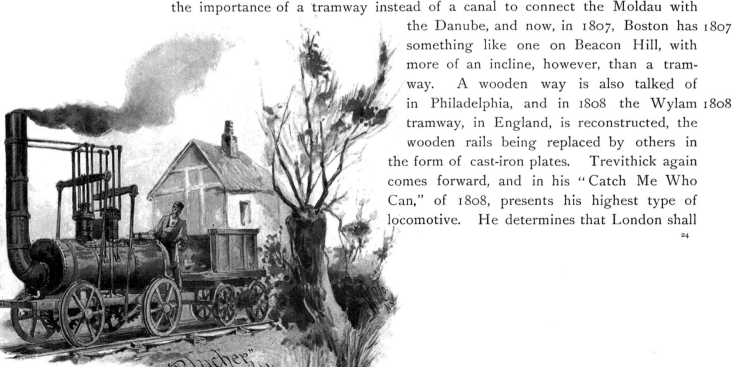

"Blucher" 1814

have an ocular demonstration of what he has done, and so takes the engine there, builds a temporary circular track, fences in a section of an unoccupied field, and, at a shilling a head, tries for the first time to make his locomotives a source of revenue. This engine, like its predecessors, is mounted on four wheels, the boiler being of the horizontal type, four feet ten inches in diameter and eight feet long, with one large return flue. The fire door and the stack are at the same end and there is one vertical double-acting cylinder fourteen inches in diameter and with a four foot stroke, and inserted in the top of the boiler in front. A wide cross-head reaches across the engine, with connecting rods extending down to crank pins in the outside of the rear wheels, which are the drivers, the forward pair being carriers only. The valve for the admission and the exhausting of steam is a four-way cock, the handle of which runs in a slot in a rod attached to the cross-head, which moves the handle up and down, changing the direction of the steam. The exhaust is into the stack, the exhaust pipe being surrounded by a chamber, into which the feed water is forced and heated on its way to the boiler. A pump is provided on the left side and worked from a lever attached to the cross-head. All four wheels are six feet in diameter. The weight is about ten tons and the speed reached on the circular track from twelve to fifteen miles an hour. For three or four weeks the engine is operated with varying success, finally a rail breaks, the engine is derailed, and Trevithick, out of money, discouraged and sick at heart, gives up. Penniless, he pathetically says: "I have been branded with folly and madness for attempting what the world calls impossibilities, even by the great engineer, James Watt, who said that I deserved hanging for bringing into use for the locomotive high-pressure steam. This, so far, has been my reward from the public. However much I may be straitened in pecuniary circumstances, the great honor of being a useful subject can never be taken from me, and which to me far exceeds riches."

In 1809, the Leiper tramway in Philadelphia is completed under

1809 the direction of John Thompson, and the same year Oliver Evans, in repeated public addresses, advocates the building of a railway from Philadelphia to New York. He vainly attempts to form a company to this end and declares "the present generation will use canals, the next will prefer railroads with horses, but their more enlightened successors will employ steam carriages on railways as the perfection of the art of conveyance."

25

In England Trevithick's fate in attempting to insure locomotion by steam has had a chilling effect, and not until 1811 is there a movement to take up the great work where he had left off, and even then it is backward instead of forward. Blenkinsop's patent for a rack railway, to obviate the slipping of the wheels, is immediately followed by the construction of a locomotive on this principle. The Blenkinsop is mounted on four wheels, has a horizontal single-flue boiler, has two vertical cylinders extending into the top of the boiler and long cross-heads reaching over the boiler transversely. To-each end of this cross-head a connecting rod is attached, reaching down by the side of the boiler to a crank on one end of each of two shafts beneath the framing and fastened thereto by boxes. On the center of each shaft there is a spur gear running into an intermediate gear located on a shaft which occupies a central position under the machine, the same height as the two shafts connected with the engine. On the extreme left end of this central shaft and outside of the road wheels there is a large toothed pinion, which gears into a rack laid on one side of the roadway, outside of the regular track, and the rack and its pinion, worked by the engine, are the means of propulsion. Several of these engines are introduced on the Middleton Colliery tramway, near Leeds, and they thus became the first type of locomotive in actual commercial use in the world. Although, owing to the power being all on one side, their movements are awkward, and the friction is largely increased, still they haul twenty or more loaded cars at an average speed of three miles an hour. Blenkinsop turns his waste steam into a small tank to deaden the noise, and from thence it passes into the open air. Matthew Murray, of Leeds, who patented the shot slide valve, is, however, the actual inventor of the rack engine, Blenkinsop being the owner of the colliery.

The Chapmans the same year obtain a patent for a method of working a locomotive engine by means of a chain stretched along the whole length of a tram road secured at each end, the engine having a grooved pulley, around which the chain is wound as the engine moves along. A locomotive on this plan is built for the Heaton Colliery, near Newcastle, but is not found practicable. This engine is on six wheels, the first time the number is increased above four, and provision is made through patent secured for the use of two four-wheel trucks, or eight wheels in all if

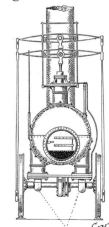

Steam Springs
1816

necessary. Only the six-wheel machine is built, however, and it is so clumsy that it is a failure for the purposes intended.

By this time there is something over one hundred and fifty miles of tramways in South Wales connecting the various collieries with canals, etc. The third road in America, at Falling Creek, Virginia, is also in operation, being about a mile in length, with wooden rails, one grooved and the other tongued; upon these rails a large wagon, with low wheels of a form to correspond with the rails, is operated by an endless rope. John Stevens, of New Jersey, applies to the Legislature of that State for a charter to build a railroad, his efforts to induce the New York authorities to construct a railroad instead of a canal to connect the eastern and western parts of the State having been ignored by the State Commissioners. Stevens, undaunted, continues his agita-
1812 tion, and in 1812 publishes a pamphlet in which he declares it a possibility to draw trains of carriages at twenty to thirty miles an hour, and that as a matter of fact he can see nothing to hinder a steam carriage moving on rails with the velocity of a hundred miles an hour.

In all the United Kingdom there is not so enterprising a colliery owner as Christopher Blackett, and in 1812 he not only has his tramway at Wylam altered to accommodate the Blenkinsop rack locomotive, but also shapes it up to enable the operation thereon of the Trevithick type of engines. He is not the sort of man to give up at one failure, or a dozen, for that matter. Almost any other man would have gone back to horses after his experience with a machine claimed to be built upon the Trevithick plan. This engine will not move an inch when expected to do so, and finally, after being coaxed, bullied and prodded by the workmen, incontinently blows up. Next he tries the Blenkin-sop style of procedure, with improvements in the way of a fly-wheel, and, while the thing moves, it almost requires a mag-   nifying glass to detect the
motion.   More horses are required   to keep it upon the track
than would be necessary to propel   the load the engine is supposed to haul, and while its end is   not the same as that of its
predecessor, it might as well be, for   there is little difference
between blowing up and being thrown over   the bank, as the outcome is the same so far as usefulness is
concerned.

A new candidate for locomotive hon-
1813 ors appears in 1813, and his scheme

27

is to overcome the want of adhesion, which all seem to think almost if not quite insurmountable by a locomotive which will through the operation of its own engine propel itself. Brunton, of the Butterley Iron Works, is the inventor, and the locomotive is a four-wheeler carrying a horizontal boiler with one tube straight through it, the fire door at one end and the chimney at the other. There is one cylinder, which is partially inserted into the boiler horizontally on the outside at the fire door end. The piston rod passes through both heads of the cylinder, front and back. At the back end it joins one of two walking, or pushing, legs, and at the front end carries a rack which works into the lower side of a pinion. Above the pinion, and engaging with it, is another rack which extends back and joins the other walking leg. The legs are each attached to the long end of a right-angle arm, which arm at the angle is attached to a horizontal arm pivoted to a stationary upright, erected from the rear end of the boiler. The short end of the angled arm carries a cord down to the leg to raise it from the ground at the end of the stroke. The Mechanical Traveler—as Brunton calls it—moves along at the rate of two and a half miles an hour and has a tractive force of four horse power. Its step is twenty-six inches long with a boiler pressure of forty to forty-five pounds to the square inch. One of these engines has been tried at the Crick Lime Works and another at the New Bottle Colliery with indifferent results in effecting a saving compared with the cost of horses.

William Hedley, Blackett's right-hand man at Wylam, evidently does not share the opinions of most people who have been insisting that smooth wheels will not afford sufficient adhesion to a smooth track. While others have been devising all sorts of contrivances to keep locomotive wheels from slipping, Hedley has been studying and figuring upon a demonstration of adhesion simply by distribution of weight. So in 1813 he builds his testing carriage, or truck,  merely a framework mounted on four wheels, the propelling power being through a system of geared wheels so arranged as to be operated by four levers worked by two men each. Upon this he loads a lot of iron blocks and bars, places his men in position, and with two or three loaded coal wagons commences the first careful and practical experiments, determining before he is through the proportion of weight required for adhesion to that of the load drawn. Others may have used smooth wheels and may have secured traction, but nobody up to this time has made the great essential a study with anything like an adequate conception of its importance, and Hedley, realizing how much he has accomplished, discards all previous ideas of locomotive construction in this direction, and straightway starts in to build the "Puffing Billy" upon the principles he has just proven to be correct. It has four flangeless wheels, the rail, or rather plates, of the Wylam line having the flange upon them. The boiler is horizontal, with a return flue, the fire door and chimney, or smoke stack, being at the front end. There are two vertical cylinders placed against the outside of the boiler at the back end, each connected to a walking beam overhead, the piston rods being connected direct to the beam without the intervention of a connecting rod or cross-head. The beams are supported by a rod at the front end pivoted at its lower end to enable the rod to swing with the movement of the beam. At the back end the beam is carried on a horizontal radial link forming a parallel motion. The connecting rods take hold between the piston rods and the front supporting link, but nearer the piston rod, and, extending down, are coupled to a crank on a shaft reaching across the engine. On the center of this shaft is a gear, engaging a gear on each of the road wheels. The valves are actuated from the beam by rods which extend to horizontal arms connected to the valve stems, there being a fulcrum between the stems and the rods, and a handle beyond the stems for the use of the engineer in operating the valves by hand. The rods from the beams are provided with two adjustable collars, one above and the other below the horizontal arm, and as the arm moves up and down it comes in contact with these collars and operates the valve. A pump on the left hand side worked from the beam supplies water to the boiler. The steam is exhausted into a common chamber located about midway on top of the boiler, and from this chamber it goes into the stack. The purpose of the chamber is to obviate the noise and pulsations in the exhaust. The "Billy" with about fifty pounds steam pressure hauls eight to ten loaded coal wagons at the rate of five miles an hour, doing with comparative ease

Burstall & Hill
1824

the work of ten horses. A decrease of the diameter of the chimney, or smoke stack, is found very advantageous, by increasing the draught to a marked extent.

Oliver Evans, who is irrepressible in his advocacy of the rail road, declares in 1813, "The time will come when people will travel in stages moved by steam engines from one city to another almost as fast as birds fly, fifteen or twenty miles an hour. A carriage will set out from Washington in the morning, the passengers will breakfast at Baltimore, dine at Philadelphia and sup in New York the same day. To accomplish this, two sets of rail ways will be laid, so nearly level as not in any place to deviate more than two degrees from the horizontal line, made of wood or iron or smooth paths of broken stone or gravel, with a rail to guide the carriages so that they may pass each other in different directions, and travel by night as well as by day, and the passengers will sleep in these stages as comfortably us they do now in steam stage boats." John Stevens, too, is full of the idea and replete with facts and figures as to cost of building railroads, which he reckons at nearly $11,000 a mile. His plan is a timber road covered with iron bar plates and elevated from three to five or six feet above the surface of the ground, to be supported by brick columns four hundred to the mile.

George Stephenson is a good deal about the place where Hedley conducts his experiments and builds his locomotive. Stephenson also makes it his rule to learn of the things going on in other places where various appliances and devices are being toyed with, as it were, in the belief that something may come of them. As to results he is probably the best posted man in that section of the country, and it is not at all strange that in 1814 he concludes to build a locomotive himself. He is a fine mechanic, and nothing impresses him more with the possibilities of the locomotive than the realization of the imperfect work done at Wylam in overhauling and attempting to improve the early Blenkinsop and Blackett designs. Stephenson commences with good financial backers, Lord Ravensworth and his partners putting up the money requisite for the inauguration of the work at the West Moor Shops of the Killingworth Colliery. He is apparently in doubt as to the desirability of turning the exhaust into the chimney, and he directs it into the open air. He also ignores Hedley's demonstration of the adhesion of smooth wheels to the smooth rails, and the " Blucher," when it first appears, has

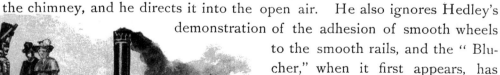

wheels closely following the Trevithick idea—in other words, roughened with bolt heads and other protuberances, to make them take hold. Otherwise the " Blucher " is not a pronounced departure from the Hedley type, and, to tell the truth, is not an overwhelming success. It makes so much noise by the escapement of steam into the atmosphere that the officers of the law give warning that the nuisance must be abated, and Stephenson turns the exhaust into the smoke stack, which results in doubling the engine's generation of steam. The roughened wheels so wrack and wrench the locomotive as to keep it constantly out of repair, and smooth wheels are substituted. Finally the " Blucher " is shaped up to draw eight loaded wagons at a speed of about three miles an hour, but is confessedly inferior to both the Blenkinsop and Hedley engines in point of efficiency and economy as compared with horse power.

Hedley, finding the " Puffing Billy's " weight on four wheels is greatly detrimental to the track, the plates breaking to an extent requiring incessant care, hits upon the plan of distribution of weight by decreasing it on the wheels, doubles the number of the latter, and thus experimentally produces the first eight-wheeler. It has two four-wheel trucks, but both are rigid, that is to say, neither is swiveling. The water is carried on another, or fifth, pair of wheels, the frames of the engine and the tank, or water carrier, being also held together rigidly. The eight-wheel plan not proving wholly satisfactory, the four-wheel style is returned to, and the plates of the roadway strengthened to 1815 meet the requirements. Stephenson, in 1815, builds his second locomotive, retaining the vertical cylinders immersed within the boiler, but each piston rod is secured to a long cross-head spanning the whole width of the engine, and having a pair of connecting rods working downward and turning one pair of wheels by means of crank pins fixed in their arms. The wheels are coupled together by a pair of rods working on pins camed by cranks forged in the axles. He has a tender for the water, and the adhesion of its wheels is obtained by coupling them to one pair of the engine wheels by means of an endless chain. In this locomotive Stephenson applies his ball and socket joint to the connecting rods, where they are attached to the piston and crank pins on the crank axles. In such way he

31

Opening Stockton & Darlington R.R. 1825

First Coach S & D 1825

overcomes somewhat the trouble upon the uneven road caused by the rigidity of the machinery. The changes made in the engine are so numerous as to render it almost impossible to keep track of them, one thing suggesting another until she is practically a half-dozen different kinds of locomotive, a sort of mechanical crazy quilt, as it were. While this is going on there is a general stirring up among those who are giving attention to the question of the future—or, rather, the present—of the locomotive. Hedley quite naturally dislikes the reflections upon his type of engine caused by Stephenson's practical failure with his first engine, in which his is so largely copied. The second Stephenson locomotive is not much better than the first, and both makers are greatly disturbed at the impatience of the public over the terrible racket kept up when the engines are under steam. Horses are frightened, good people made nervous, and the situation, with its wrangles, its jealousies and complications generally, is not a pleasant one.

Dodd, who is working with Stephenson, and probably suggested the ball and socket joint, has also a plan to get rid of the cumbrous wheels and pinions, as well as the jerks and concussions, and he and Stephenson together take out a patent including the ball and socket joint and the application of a pin on one of the spokes of the wheels supporting the engine, the lower end of the connecting rod being attached thereto by the ball and socket joint. The next year, 1816, 1816 Stephenson gets to work on his third locomotive, introducing in it the steam springs, protected by the letters patent taken out by Dodd and himself. It is his purpose to ease the weight of the engine upon the axles, without at the same time permitting any vertical motion of the boiler other than of the wheels themselves in rising and falling according to the inequalities of the track; so he holds a portion of the weight of the engine upon a piston contained in vertical cylinders beneath and communicating freely with the interior of the boiler, the pistons being made to press downward upon the bearings of the axles. But the arrange-

ment proves defective in principle, and is objectionable on the score of leakage, wear and tear, etc., and is soon abandoned. Losh and Stephenson also give some attention to the improvement of the track, and in 1816 take out a patent for a form of rail and chair. The joinings of the rails with each other are

Locomotion 1825

accomplished by a half lap, the sides of the tops of the rails being beveled away near the ends for about two inches and a half, so that when the two beveled ends are laid against each other they form the same breadth of surface as the top of the rail in other parts. One pin-hole passes through the two ends, and through a single hole in the chair a strong iron pin is driven, which keeps the ends of the rails from separating.

A Quaker named Pease proposes in 1817 to build a line of road in England from Stockton to Darlington, some thirty-seven miles, for the carrying of coal. In 1818 the fourth tramway in the United States is laid in Armstrong County, Pennsylvania; it has wooden rails and extends from the Bear Creek furnace to navigation. In 1819 a party by the name of Dearborn, in Boston, forwards a memorial to Congress advocating the construction of railways, which he declares should "have carriages provided with accommodations for passengers to take their meals and their rest during passage. Protection from the attacks of assailants," he says, "will be insured, not only by the celerity of the movement, but by weapons of defence belonging to the carriage." The same year the Hetton Colliery, near Sunderland, in England, is altered into a road capable of bearing locomotives, and George Stephenson is made Chief Engineer and given authority to go ahead and build several engines.

The "Stevens"
1825

1819 also marks the end of all things earthly to Oliver Evans, the destruction by fire of the works erected by him in Philadelphia, and in which he invested his entire means, breaking his heart. John Stevens survives him, and is petitioning the Legislature of Pennsylvania to authorize the construction of a railroad from Philadelphia to Pittsburgh.

In England Thomas Gray, in 1820, jumps into the agitation of the use of steam for all character of land conveyance with a vim that creates much discussion. He is so energetic and pertinacious that the Edinburgh Review declares him mad, and that he should be shut up in Bedlam. Gray certainly wakes things up, if nothing more. While he is doing this on one side of the Atlantic, Stevens, not to be put down by the indifference of Congress and Legislatures to his appeals to recognize the advantages of railways, builds a short line on his own property at Hoboken, and at his own expense, to experiment upon. The track is laid on a true plane, but in-

33

Gurney's Steam Carriage
1825

clined on one side on stone pillars, so as to be about thirty inches higher than the opposite side. It is upon wooden stringers capped with iron. There is a cast-iron rack laid in the center of the track with teeth into which a cog or tooth wheel upon the engine will gear.

Malleable iron rails in England, up to this time, have not been much used, as from the narrowness of their heads they cause great injury to the wheels, and the overcoming of this by increasing their breadth so augments the cost as to exceed that of cast iron. John Birkinshaw, of the Bedlington Iron Works, has, however, through a patent just taken out, brought about a decided change in the order of things. He not only produces a rail of the same bearing surface as the cast iron, but through the machinery he has also invented rolls them in lengths of fifteen feet, or if necessary eighteen feet. This is a decided advance, for the cast-iron rails can only be made three or four feet long, require frequent joints, and have a great tendency to break, especially under heavy weights. Despite the efforts of Stephenson and his friends, and notwithstanding Stephenson's demonstration with his locomotives on the Killingworth and on the Hetton roads, the determination not to use locomotives on the Newcastle and Carlisle road remains unchanged, and horse power is decided to be preferable, both from the point of efficiency and of economy.

For some little time it has been apparent that the matter of applying steam for stage coach travel is securing a hold on inventors. The main obstacle appears to be that the boilers in use on the railways cannot be adapted to common roads, and the necessity is imperative that a new and light type of boiler must come before the steam carriage will materialize. Julius Griffiths, in 1821, 1821 has his plans so perfected as to enable the construction of the pioneer locomotive steam coach, as he terms it. It has two working steam cylinders, which, together with the boiler, a condenser and other appendages, are suspended to a frame at the back of the vehicle, which in the main is a double coach with capacity for eight passengers. The boiler is not of sufficient size to enable continuous work, but the carriage moves easily, and is guided with little or no trouble, thus demonstrating in this, the first effort to enlarge the use of steam to passenger transport that it is perfectly feasible. Other carriages follow these experiments and they are the talk

34

of mechanical circles. Some of them are peculiar in the extreme, illustrating a variety of thought and a range of comprehension truly remarkable. David Gordon, in 1822, takes an enormous drum or cylinder, nine feet in diameter, fits a double rack into it, and then with a locomotive of the Trevithick type, mounted upon rack wheels, starts the thing in motion on pretty much the same principle a squirrel sets his tin wheel spinning. Goldsworthy Gurney, the same year, uses ammoniacal gas to a purpose. Meantime, the Hetton Colliery road—in course of a radical alteration, for steam power is nearing completion—in November is opened with five of George Stephenson's locomotives, each drawing seventeen wagons, or an average aggregate of sixty-four tons, at the rate of four miles an hour. Within a month or two three of these locomotives are discarded, and fixed engines employed in their stead. The other two are recommended for condemnation, and a return to horse power is contemplated.

John Roger's Suggestion
B&O 1827

1822 In 1822 the Liverpool and Manchester Railroad is projected by William James, and the following year the proposed line is surveyed by Charles Vignoles. 1823 marks the first fruition of John Stevens' long struggle to gain recognition in the United States, the Legislature of Pennsylvania author-
1823 izing the construction of a railroad line from Philadelphia to the Susquehanna, but refusing the authority asked for to build to Pittsburgh. George Stephenson decides to accept the offer to go to the Stockton and Darlington road as its engineer, the line being under construction without the slightest thought, primarily, on the part of its promoters that steam would be used to the exclusion of horse power.

1824 W. H. James, in London, in 1824, is one of the most active of those devoting time and money to the solving of the many-sided question as to the best form of boiler and machinery for the new style of passenger propulsion, the steam carriage. His patent is a pronounced departure, inasmuch as instead of actuating the several wheels with one engine he adapts a separate one for each, the idea being that in this way he can turn corners and otherwise manipulate the carriage to a greater advantage. Burstall and Hill also produce an entirely new design in steam carriages, in the form of a machine having a conical boiler supported on an iron frame, extending from the second to the third pair of wheels. High-pressure steam is used and two cylinders are employed. Gordon, too, comes forward with a new

35

Royal George
1827

scheme, in a three-wheel steam carriage, the propelling power being six hollow iron legs, with feet at the lower extremities, so placed and so acting as to walk or push the machine along when under steam.

The prospectus of the Liverpool and Manchester Railway is out, and it is the first in England proposed for the general railroad business, all others up to this time having contemplated the transportation simply of a single commodity, coal or stone, and being operated merely as adjuncts to a colliery, a quarry or the like. But the Liverpool and Manchester is to be a public, not a private enterprise; a general, not an individual concern. George Washington Smith proposes a line of railway from Baltimore to the Ohio, and endorses John Stevens' plan before the Pennsylvania Legislature for the road from Philadelphia to Pittsburgh.

Wrought-iron plate rails are taking the place of those of cast iron, and coming quite largely into use in the collieries in the north of England. Before Stephenson leaves Killingworth, in 1825, he completes his improved Killingworth locomotive, in which he abandons entirely the endless chain, substituting therefor outside coupling rods, which connect the front and rear wheels. Springs are by him first introduced in this engine, and it also marks an innovation in the position of the cylinders, and a compacting of the locomotive to a better form, getting rid of a host of rods and joints.

Stephenson has become the engineer of the Stockton and Darlington, and it is opened September 27th, 1825, with one of his engines, the "Locomotion," the hand bill, as the advanced announcement of the event, uniquely describing it as "The Company's Locomotive Engine and the Engine's Tender." George Stephenson himself officiates as the engineer of the "Locomotion." Its boiler contains a single straight flue, one end of which is the furnace. The cylinders are vertical, like those of his earlier engines, and are coupled directly to the driving wheels. The crank pins are set in the wheels at right angles. The two pairs of drivers are coupled by horizontal rods, and the exhaust is into the stack. Timothy Hackworth, who has been with Stephenson for some time at his locomotive factory at Newcastle, and is now with him on the Stockton and Darlington as the locomotive engineer, designed the wheels of the engine "Locomotion," this accounting for the fact that they are so entirely different from anything Stephenson has hitherto had in his engines. It is not without much hesitation, and in the face of very

36

Stephenson's Twin Sisters 1827

serious opposition, that the line is opened with steam power, and only three of Stephenson's locomotives have been ordered. The construction is for horse power, and no provision has been made for permanent operation otherwise; still, the opening is productive of no ordinary enthusiasm, and on every hand there are predictions that the iron horse has at last come to stay. The car containing the directors of the company on the opening of the road, and attached to the rear of the train of coal cars, is an old stage coach body taken off of its usual supports, mounted upon a framework, supported by the wheels taken from under a coal car or wagon. It is named the "Experiment," and passes into history as the first type of railway passenger coach. It belongs to a stage coach line, the managers of which have made an arrangement with the Stockton and Darlington Company to run it upon the road with the provision that the side track shall always be taken when a train of coal wagons comes in view. Passengers are carried at so much each, the same as on the stage line, and it is drawn by horses, as the locomotive service is exclusively for freight.

The steam carriage builders keep on with their plans, specifications and patents, and hardly a week passes without some new idea being broached, some new scheme of propulsion figured out, or an old one improved upon. Possibly under the latter classification will come Gurney's combination of legs and levers in his carriage, it being proposed to use the former when going up hill or where the wheels will not take hold, the arrangement being such that when the wheels slip the legs, or propellers, come into action.

In America Smith and Stevens are having an extended discussion as to the comparative cost of building the lines to the Ohio and to Pittsburgh. Stevens having completed his little experimental railway at Hoboken, builds in 1825 a small locomotive to demonstrate the truth of some of his claims in this practical manner. The engine has a single cylinder exactly horizontal, it resting on the main frame, and is four and a half inches in diameter, with one foot stroke. The boiler is formed of a number of vertical tubes each 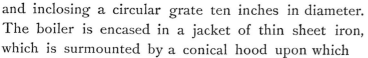 one and a quarter inches external diameter and four and a half feet long. These tubes are set closely together in a circle surrounding and inclosing a circular grate ten inches in diameter. The boiler is encased in a jacket of thin sheet iron, which is surmounted by a conical hood upon which

Hancock's Steam Wagon 1827

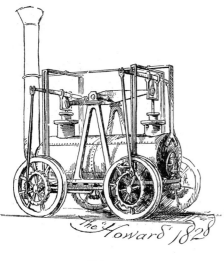

The "Howard" 1828

Liverpool & Manchester 1828

the smoke stack rests. The fuel is wood and is dropped on the grate through a door in the hood. The engine is on four wheels of four feet diameter, and moves at a rate of two miles an hour.

In 1826 the Wilsons of Newcastle build a locomotive for the Stockton and 1826 Darlington road with four cylinders, two to each pair of wheels. The same year Stephenson completes a locomotive for the company with six coupled wheels, outside inclined cylinders, the boiler containing two fire tubes, and the exhaust steam being conveyed from the cylinders to the chimney by two blast pipes, one for each cylinder.

The range of means proposed for land propulsion by steam appears to be without limit. Seaward invents a plan whereby the wheels are mounted upon a swing frame to correct unevenness of the ground, and the wheels have projecting teeth to hold on with. James perfects a mechanism through which a universal joint communicates rotary motion to each successive carriage in a railway train, so it will pass around curves up to thirty degrees without friction. Easton thinks to get his carriage along by raising the middle of the road way, laying thereon a rack or toothed bar of iron, with a corresponding rack or toothed wheel revolved by steam in the vehicle itself. Fisher wants to suspend his carriages on a double line of rail instead of, as Palmer suggests, having but one rail and the body of the carriage on both sides of it. Hill is to have the flanges on his wheels adjustable, so that when his railway carriages are used on common roads there will be no difficulty on this score. He also contemplates having the wheels revolve loosely upon fixed axles, and making railway rails tubes instead of solid iron, to save metal and obtain strength. Brown runs a carriage up hill at a lively rate with a gas vacuum engine, and Viney and Pocock employ a kite attached to a phaeton as a means of propulsion with such success that they secure a patent on the plan, adding a provision for a platform on wheels, with the view of carrying a small pony to meet such an emergency as a calm or unusually light wind. Snowden arranges to carry his horses aboard his machine and have them furnish the power of propulsion there instead of in the usual way. Neville invents a series of springing plates to go upon the tires of the wheels of his carriage and through this form of pro-

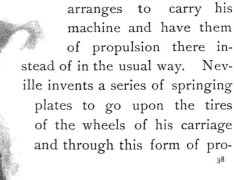

Johnson's Steam Wagon 1828

38

jection in contact with the ground enhance adhesion, while Holland adapts the "lazy-tong" principle as a means of deriving reciprocating motion. There are evidently many men of many minds on land transit just at this time and a far greater activity in steam carriage than in locomotive circles.

A line of wooden rail resting upon granite sleepers is commenced in 1826 at the granite quarries in Quincy, Massachusetts, and is to extend three miles to the Neponset River. Another road of similar character, excepting that the rails are upon wooden instead of granite sleepers, or sills, is being constructed at Pottsville, Pennsylvania. The Pennsylvania Legislature grants charters for a rail road from the Lackawaxen to the Lackawanna, and for another road from Pottsville to the Susquehanna.

France authorizes her first railway early in 1826, the St. Etienne and Lyons, and it is but a few months later when Marc Seguin, the engineer of the road, commences a series of experiments which prove him a man of no ordinary brightness and adaptability. He purchases an old locomotive of Stephenson's make, simply as a basis for his operations, and which by the time he has it ready

Knight
Horse Locomotive
1829

1827 for a trial, in 1827, the original inventor cannot recognize. The boiler is the point of the most radical changes, as from it he removes the single flue and in its place inserts such as brings about the first application of the multitubular principle in locomotive construction in the world. Finding the draught defective, he introduces a fan in connection with the tender, so arranging it that with the revolution of the wheels he secures the desired result. The "Seguin," as the engine is named, has two vertical cylinders, one on each side, located centrally between the wheels and fastened to the boiler. The piston rod connects direct to the center of an overhead beam and at each end of the beam a connecting rod is secured, the rods being attached to crank pins in the wheels. The alignment of the piston rod is secured by a parallel motion. The steam chest is at the back of the cylinder, and the valve is worked from the overhead beam by a rod extending down to a lever attached to the valve stem.

Baltimore is becoming more than ordinarily agitated over the situation in her circles of trade, consequent upon the results of the completion of the Erie Canal. Philadelphia and New York are dividing up the business between them and Baltimore is threatened with a decline of commercial importance of the most serious nature.

39

Rocket 1829

B&O Strap Rail 1829

Philip E. Thomas, President of the Mechanics' Bank, and George Brown, one of the directors, have several conferences. The outcome is the resignation of Thomas as a Commissioner of the State for the Chesapeake and Ohio Canal, on the ground that as a practical channel for the transportation of either merchandise or passengers to and from the West it will prove abortive, so far, at least, as any advantage can be derived from it by Baltimore. This leaves Thomas free to act as he pleases, and, with Brown working with him, they speedily develop an interest that leads to the holding of a meeting at Brown's residence in Baltimore, which is attended by well-known merchants and financiers, and at which the question of the construction of a railroad to connect the navigable waters of Chesapeake Bay with those of the Ohio is thoroughly discussed. This is in February, 1827, and, appointing a committee of the best known men of the city, the meeting adjourns for a week. Reassembling, Thomas, as Chairman of the Committee, reads a very able paper on the advantages of railroads over canals and waterways generally. Business is evidently the watchword of these Baltimoreans, for without further parley, and with a promptness showing the metal these men are made of, a resolution is unanimously passed "That immediate application be made to the Legislature of Maryland for an act incorporating a joint stock company to be styled the 'Baltimore and Ohio Railway Company,' and clothing such company with all powers necessary for the construction of a railroad with two or more sets of rails from the city of Baltimore to the Ohio River." The capital stock of the company is fixed at $5,000,000. A committee, with Charles Carroll, of Carrollton, at its head, is appointed to secure a charter, and in nine days thereafter this is perfected. In less than two months the company is duly organized, with Philip E. Thomas as its President and George Brown, Treasurer. Preparations are at once made for a survey, this work being entrusted to Colonel Stephen H. Long, of the United States Topographical Corps, and Jonathan Knight.

The usual width of the wooden and cast-iron tramways in England practically determines the gauge of the new lines. They are quite generally about five feet over all—that is, including the width of the two rails—and as Jessop's edge rail and the Killingworth rails are one and three-quarter inches wide, the width of the two rails

Ackworth's Sans Pareil 1829

"Evan Thomas" 1829

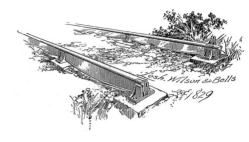

Fish, Wilson & Bells
1829

The "Cyclopede"
1829

1827 of track deducted from five feet leaves four feet eight and a half inches as the standard gauge, so to speak, with the fish belly of fifteen feet length as the standard rail. The signal used by engineers for stopping a train is a burning tow line kindled by a shovelfull of red-hot cinders; a candle stuck in the window is the signal to stop, and its absence means to go on. The chilling of the wheels of locomotives is deemed objectionable as diminishing the adhesion upon the rails, and so the common cast-iron wheels continue to be generally used. Experiments made with rims or tires of wrought iron are said to have produced satisfactory results.

The four-cylinder engine built by Wilson & Co. for the Stockton and Darlington road is not a success, and going through a collision has not improved it. Timothy Hackworth, the locomotive engineer of the company, determines to rebuild it, and obtains the assent of the directors to do so only after a good deal of persuasion. The four Stephenson locomotives on the road are not regarded with favor and the experience with steam power has been such that the company is inclined to abandon it altogether. But Hackworth is persistent, and the " Royal George," as he re-christens the Wilson engine, comes forth so radically changed as to create remark. It has a cistern into which a portion of the exhaust steam is turned to heat the feed water, short stroke force pumps working by eccentrics, adjustable springs instead of weights upon the safety valves, and a single lever reversing gear. The cylinders are eleven inches in diameter, with a twenty inch stroke. Throwing the steam into the chimney through a single blast orifice greatly augments the force of the steam blast, and consequently the combustion in the furnace. This is done, indeed, to an extent never before attempted, and is practically the first introduction of the steam blast upon a carefully calculated principle and with a full comprehension of its advantages.

Stephenson builds the same year the locomotive " Twin Sisters " for the use of the contractors on the Liverpool and Manchester Railway. As it is required to work over severe temporary gradients, it is regarded best to construct it with twin boilers in order to insure water at all times covering the top of the fire boxes. This engine is upon six wheels, four feet in diameter, and all coupled, the cylinders being placed on an incline. There are two blast pipes,

41

Ericsson's "Novelty"
1829

one for each cylinder. Walter Hancock, who has for some time been working 1827 on a boiler with a special view to its use in steam carriages for common roads, brings out his first vehicle. It is upon three wheels, the power is applied through the medium of two vibrating or oscillating engines fixed upon the crank axle of the fore wheel. Although not equalling expectations, it traverses the ordinary roads with fair speed and has covered several hundred miles.

The Mauch Chunk Railroad is completed and forms the largest and most important line of the character existent in the United States. It commences at the coal mines in the valley of the Little Schuylkill, is nine miles in length, with branches aggregating nearly four additional miles, is used exclusively for transporting coal and is an incline plane rather than a railway as the latter term is beginning to be understood. The rails are of timber laid on wooden sleepers and strapped with flat iron bars. The Mill Creek Railroad, from Mine Hill to Port Carbon, Pennsylvania, is also in operation. The main line is some four miles in length, with six turnouts. There are nine branch lines, aggregating five miles of trackage. The rails are of white oak, five by three and a half inches, fastened to round chestnut sleepers eight to ten inches in diameter, notched and wedged on the outside. The whole rests simply upon the natural soil, with no attempt at a road bed. Horatio Allen, who has been connected with the Delaware and Hudson Canal Company for some time, has resigned in order to visit England and makes an investigation of railroad progress. The canal people have arranged with him to contract for the rails for their contemplated coal road and also for three locomotives, and this is the initial commercial recognition of locomotive power on the American continent.

John Rogers, of Baltimore, in conjunction with Benjamin H. Latrobe, of the same city, publishes a pamphlet advocating the use of steam on the Baltimore and Ohio Railroad, and it contains an engraving of a type of locomotive believed to be applicable, being the first suggested power of the character for a railroad in the United States. The idea is to lay a rack rail, with a corresponding wheel on the locomotive, so that by the operation of its steam power the engine will work itself onward. Late in the year the Legislature of South Carolina

Stourbridge Lion 1829

James 1829

42

grants a charter for the Charleston and Hamburg Railroad, one hundred and thirty-six miles in length.

1828 In 1828 the Johnson Brothers, who have a small engineering establishment in Philadelphia, complete and put upon the streets the first steam wagon built and actually operated as such in the United States. It has a single cylinder set horizontally with a connecting rod attachment to a single crank at the middle of the driving axle. Its two driving wheels are eight feet in diameter and made of wood, the same as those on an ordinary road wagon. The two forward or guiding wheels are much smaller than the others, and are arranged in the usual manner of a common wagon. It has an upright boiler hung on behind, shaped like a huge bottle, the smoke stack coming out through the center of the top. The safety valve is held down by a weight and lever, and the horses in the neighborhood do not take kindly to the puffing of the machine as it jolts over the rough streets. It has knocked down a number of awning posts, broken several window fronts, and at times is so unmanageable as to be a menace to the good Quaker peace of mind. Otherwise it runs well and surmounts considerable elevations in the streets and roadways.

Improved Car on S&D
1829

Long and Knight, the engineers who have been making the survey for the line of the Baltimore and Ohio Railroad, report early in April proposing various routes ; and that along the valley of the Patapsco, and thence to Point of Rocks on the Potomac is decided upon. This line is accordingly located, the right of way secured, and preparations made to commence work by the laying of the cornerstone on the anniversary of the nation's Independence, with ceremonies unparalleled in the history of the country. The venerable Charles Carroll, of Carrollton, the last surviving signer of the Declaration of Independence, and now upward of ninety years of age, is invited to lay the cornerstone, and not only Baltimore, but the whole State of Maryland is in a perfect fever of excitement. The day is glorious, the weather all that can be desired, the city is decorated as never a city was before, and the procession is a remarkable one, embracing in its many divisions every trade, industry and organization of the municipality and commonwealth. There does not appear to be a man, woman or child capable of going on foot, in wagon, carriage or cart, or horseback, muleback, and even astride a steer or ox, who is not at the

Sail Car
So Carolina R.R.
1829

43

Stephenson's "America"
1829

scene when the stone marking the actual beginning of the first railroad in the
real sense of the term on the American continent is most impressively conse-
crated. Within three days the definite location of the line is begun, and a week
later notice is publicly given that proposals will be received for the grading and
masonry on the first twelve miles. Trouble with the Chesapeake and Ohio Canal
Company at once ensues over the question as to pre-emption rights, but the railroad people push ahead their plans with such energy that, by the 1st of October,
President Thomas reports that the contractors have all commenced their labors
and are rapidly advancing their sections, three of which, including a distance
of one and a half miles, are ready for the rails. The Delaware and Hudson
Canal Company has completed the construction of a road from their coal mines
at Carbondale to Honesdale, Pennsylvania, the terminus of their canal. Horatio
Allen, who is in Europe in their interest to a certain extent, gives an order to
Foster, Rastrick & Co., of Stourbridge, for two locomotives, and to the Stephensons for a third. In the construction of the road wooden piles and trestles are
being introduced as substitutes for sleepers and embankments, which is an innovation. The line is about sixteen miles in length, and a portion of it is operated by inclined planes.

Moncure Robinson's plan for roadbed is meeting with much favor, particularly on the route in course of construction in Pennsylvania. The sleepers are
deeply embedded in the ground, and thus protected from the feet of the horses
and the action of the atmosphere; square blocks of locust or other durable timber
are attached to them near their extremities, and projecting above them to the
surface. The rails rest on notches cut into these blocks, and keys or wedges
maintain them in position. William T. James, who has a shop in Eldridge
Court, New York City, has started in to build locomotives. His first effort is a
diminutive affair with cylinders, having a diameter of two and a stroke of four
inches. This engine he places upon a circular track, about twenty-five
feet in diameter, laid upon the shop floor, and attaches to it four four-
wheel cars, upon each of which is a boy. The machine moves around
with this train and load as rapidly as a man can walk. The firing of
the tiny locomotive, as a matter of course, is done before the
start, and Samuel B. Dougherty, an apprentice boy of sixteen,
is the engineer. James has just finished his second locomotive,
which is considerably larger than the
first. It is on three wheels and de-

44

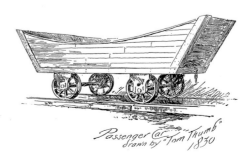

Passenger Car "Tom Thumb"
drawn by "Tom Thumb" 1830

1828 signed to run upon the floor or sidewalk instead of upon rails. The two rear wheels are the drivers and the forward the steering wheel. This engine has two cylinders of the same dimensions as the first, but they are placed upright. While James is thus making practical experiments in New York, William Howard, connected with the Engineer Corps of the Baltimore and Ohio in Baltimore, is figuring out on paper an improved locomotive, to be propelled by steam on rail or other roads. His plans and specifications are finally filed at Washington, and upon them the first patent for a locomotive is issued in the United States.

In England the great work of the Liverpool and Manchester, the first railroad for general business in Europe, is being pushed onward, and is by common opinion deemed the experiment which is to decide the fate of railways abroad. "The eyes of the whole scientific world," writes Nicholas Wood, "are upon this great undertaking; public opinion upon the subject remains suspended, and hence its progress is watched with the most intense interest." George Stephenson is at the head of the work. The gauge is four feet eight and a half inches, and the law has fixed this for all lines of public railway. Stephenson and his son, Robert, are worried over the reports that the Stockton and Darlington is to put aside its locomotives and give place to horses, and both write to Hackworth to ascertain if it is true. That this has not been done up to this period is unquestionably largely due to the successful operation of the "Royal George," the engine Hackworth remodeled, and which is demonstrating a capacity far in advance of any other locomotive in England.

The Legislature of Pennsylvania has authorized the construction of a line from Philadelphia to the Susquehanna as a State work. This is the first railroad in the world undertaken purely as a governmental enterprise.

Ross Winans, of Baltimore, who for some time has been working upon anti-friction wheels and cars, concludes to give a public demonstration in the Chamber of Commerce of that city of the results reached. He has a model of a car weighing a hundred and twenty-five pounds running upon a track In this he places five hundred

45

South Carolina R'y. 1830

pounds of iron and two men, and then draws the whole with a piece of twine. The patent he has secured covers the wheels, the axles, and the carriage or car as a whole.

Everything pertaining to the railroad is eagerly seized upon by those interested in the new lines under construction or proposed. American engineers have no experience in railroads for the general purpose of transit of persons and goods, or, for that matter, neither have the English engineers. The only roads in actual operation in America are the Mauch Chunk, nine miles long, for carrying coal by gravity and mill power ; and the Quincy, three miles long, for carrying granite by animal power. There are in fact no railroads for general purposes in operation in any part of the world. The Liverpool and Manchester Railway for the conveyance of passengers and goods is simply under construction. All others in England are for carrying coals or the products of quarries, furnaces, etc., but not for the transportation of general merchandise and passengers. The Baltimore and Ohio Railroad is for the conveyance of freight and passengers, and therefore the two short, so-called railroads, the Mauch Chunk and the Quincy, afford no model to go by regarding either track or equipment. The mechanism and running gear of the quarry and coal roads are not adapted to the transit of passengers or general freight, hence entirely new and different machinery has to be originated and built. The equipment, including the motive power machinery, has to be planned and perfected, and it can only be brought about by invention, theory and experiment. The Baltimore and Ohio, as the pioneer railroad in America, and the Liverpool and Manchester, as the pioneer in Europe, have therefore to "blaze" the way, almost as literally as the hardy foresters who were the pioneers of civilization.

The first section of rail on the Baltimore and Ohio is laid during the Winter of 1828–9, extending from Mount Clare westward about three miles. Upon it 1829 various experiments are tried, among them sails to a limited extent, but the favorite mode of conveyance is a flat car drawn by a horse. This car, devised by Ross Winans, has his anti-friction wheels, and the horse, as a consequence, is able to propel it at a speed quite exhilarating in comparison to that obtained in the usual way on the common road.

Colonel Long, in his connection with the Baltimore and Ohio, became acquainted with William Norris, a well-known business man in Baltimore, and the subjects of conversation taking a turn towards the railroad rather

46

"Northumbrian" 1830

First Enclosed Car on B&O 1830

1829 than commerce, Norris speedily loses all interest in other than the matter nearest the gallant Colonel's heart, which is that of designing and constructing a locomotive. Norris has devoted his spare hours to scientific reading, with a tendency to mechanics, and he can match the Colonel's practice with theories, so the two naturally drift the one way. The culmination is reached in 1829 in the shape of plans and specifications for a locomotive to burn anthracite coal. It has two driving wheels, five feet in diameter, placed in front of the fire-box, and outside cylinders. The front part of the engine rests in a pivoted bearing upon a four-wheel truck. The peculiarity of the boiler as proposed is in the arrangement of the tubes, there being two sets, and between them a space about twenty inches in length, which serves as a combustion chamber for the gases and smoke. There is to be attached to the boiler a fan blower driven by the exhaust steam, and operated by the engineman at his pleasure.

The pioneer railroad in Austria is completed, forty miles being opened on the first of April. The whole line, eighty miles in length, is in fact finished, from Budweis, a town in Bohemia, on the Moldau—a tributary to the Elbe—to Lurtz, in Austria, on the Danube, and it is one of, if not indeed the longest, now in the world. Its traffic consists of salt. That portion of the road in the town of Budweis is laid with cast-iron rails, all the rest being wood string-pieces resting on very long sleepers, which, in turn, rest upon a dry stone wall, five and a half feet thick.

English Coal Car
1830

All is not well on the Liverpool and Manchester railway as the time approaches for the directors to decide upon the motive power to be used, at least not for Stephenson and those who have so confidently counted upon a decision favorable to locomotives. It is true the directors ordered from Stephenson the locomotive which was placed experimentally upon the tracks of the Company early in the Winter, but it is equally true that its performance is anything but encouraging. It is of the same imperfect and unsatisfactory class as that supplied by Stephenson to the Stockton and Darlington, and as a matter of fact to its failure, as much as anything else, can be attributed the feeling of the directors in favor of almost any other power. It is now proposed to divide the road into nineteen stations, or sections, of about a mile and a half each, with twenty-one engines fixed

Stephenson's "Mercury"
1830

at the different points to work chains forward. Hardly a professional man of
any experience, George Stephenson alone excepted, can be found at this time
who prefers the locomotive rather than the fixed engine power. This illus-
trates most forcibly the popular opinion of the value of locomotives in England as based upon the performance of the eighteen Stephenson has built,
and the few others put into service by persons not so well known. America,
without any locomotives whatever, is about as well off, and probably better
so far as successful progress is concerned, for no one man has great prominence to make him the target of jealous rivals or to give him sufficient
power to hold competitors in check. Repeated failures have not resulted in
discouragement, and the hope that is said to spring eternally has had no severe
setback. Sometimes it is quite as well to make haste slowly as to rush in where
angels fear to tread. May be it is this, may be something else; but whatever it
is, the locomotive in England, with the opening of Spring, is not popular.
The more or less success the steam carriages are meeting with on common roads
is about the only bright gleam in the locomotive builders' horizon. Some of the
directors of the Liverpool and Manchester, who have stock in the steam carriage
companies, and are thoroughly posted on the subject, are unquestionably inclined
to lean toward the locomotive, in the belief that what can be done with a steam
carriage on the road ought at the least to be within the range of possibilities
with a steam locomotive on rails. A deputation of the directors visit Newcastle,
Darlington, and the neighboring collieries, but their conclusions as to the locomotives employed there are unfavorable. Walker and Rastrick, engineers of
distinction, are called in to examine the whole subject of fixed and locomotive
power, and after an exhaustive inquiry they report in favor of the stationary
engines and rope traction. This is in March, and Nicholas Wood, an eminent
authority on everything pertaining to the railroad, officially confirms the
engineers' decision. No man is better informed on the Stephenson or Newcastle
engines than Wood, and his decided convictions against their use as compared
with the fixed engines is very depres-
sing to the company's engineer, Stephenson himself. The directors of the
road are therefore upon the point of
adopting fixed engines and ropes, when,
as a last and conclusive experiment,
two or three members of the board pre-

Timothy Hackworth

Hackworth's "Globe"
1830

1829 vail upon the others to consent to a public trial of locomotives, open to all comers, for a purse of five hundred pounds. This decision is reached on the 20th of April, and on the 25th the offer is published with the following provisions : That the successful engine shall effectually consume its own smoke; if it weighs six tons it must be capable of drawing after it, day by day, on a level plane, a train of the gross weight of twenty tons, including tender and water tank, at the rate of ten miles an hour; the pressure of steam in the boiler must not exceed fifty pounds to the square inch; there must be two safety valves, one of which is to be completely out of the reach or control of the engineer, and neither of which can be fastened down; the engine and boiler must be supported on springs and rest on four wheels, and the height from the ground to the top of the chimney must not exceed fifteen feet. The length of track upon which the competition is to take place is but a mile and a half, possibly a trifle more. Each engine has to traverse this forward and backward ten times, that is, ten round trips, or thirty miles. A judge is to be stationed at each terminus of the running course, and the little additional track at each end is for getting up speed. Stephenson's "Rocket," Hackworth's "Sans Pareil," Ericsson and Braithwaite's "Novelty," Burstall's "Perseverance" and Brandreth's "Cyclopede" are the five contestants for the prize. The "Cyclopede" is operated by horse power and therefore not within the conditions. The "Perseverance" is a steam carriage, not a locomotive to run on a railroad, and is withdrawn by its inventor.

The "Rocket" has a cylindrical boiler six feet long, three feet in diameter, with flat ends. The upper half is used as a reservoir for the steam and the lower half is filled with water. Extending through this lower part there are twenty-five copper tubes, three inches in diameter, forming a passage from the fire-box to the chimney. The fire-box is two feet wide and three feet high, located immediately behind the boiler and surrounded with water. The cylinders, two in number, are placed one on each side of the boiler in an oblique position, one end being nearly even with the top of the boiler, and the other pointing toward the center of the foremost driving-wheel with which connection is made from the piston rod by a joint to the outside of the wheel. The weight of the engine is four and a half tons.

The "Sans Pareil" has two vertical cylinders, eight inches in diameter and with an eighteen inch stroke.

49

These are located just over the rear driving wheels, which are four feet in
diameter and coupled with side rods to the forward pair of wheels. The valves
are worked by two eccentrics loose on the axle, and driven by two clutches, one
being provided for running in each direction. There is also a gear for working
the valves by hand, so as to turn the engine a half revolution and bring the
right clutch into gear. The boiler has a single flue, with the fire inside of it.
The exhaust steam is used to create draft in the chimney. The "Sans Pareil"
weighs nearly four hundred pounds over the prescribed limit but is allowed
to compete on the same footing as the others.

The "Novelty," a tank engine on four wheels, is the first of the type. The
boiler is upright with a horizontal chamber, in which there is a return flue. The
bottom is closed tight, air being supplied by a bellows worked from the engine
by a bell crank. The boiler is fed from the top through an opening closed by a
slide. There are two vertical cylinders, with piston rods extending through the
upper heads and connected to cross-heads projecting over the sides a distance
sufficient to allow connecting rods to couple them direct to the horizontal arms
of a bell crank. The vertical arms of the bell cranks are connected to cranks
on the driving axle by other rods. The valves are worked by rods attached to
the cross-heads. The stack is at the front end of the engine and the exhaust is
discharged into the atmosphere.

The "Rocket" proves to be the only one of the three engines constructed
with sufficient care and durability to stand the test of operation under the
pressure of steam necessary to meet the requirements and therefore wins the
prize. It is apparent that Stephenson has a great advantage in being the only
one of the trio of locomotive builders who has a shop or factory of his own.
Hackworth has the experience and knowledge of essentials it brings, but he has
no shop facilities under his own direction of sufficient extent to enable
him to do as he pleases. He has charge, it is true, of the Stockton and
Darlington shops, but they are small and meagre, and so pressed with
the burden of work constantly neces-
sitated upon the Stephenson engines
operated by the road that it is only
between times, as it were, that Hackworth can do anything on the "Sans
Pareil." He is finally forced to have
the cylinders for his engine made by

Bury 1830

1829 one of his competitors in the trial, Stephenson, and for some reason or other no less than five are cast before the two which are placed on the locomotive are obtained. The "Sans Pareil" has hardly commenced running on the day of the trial when one of these cylinders cracks through the bore into the steam port and investigation shows that the thickness of the metal has been reduced by imperfect moulding and boring to hardly more than a sixteenth of an inch. To add to the difficulties of the situation, the feed pump fails, and the blast is so powerful that the coke is thrown out of the stack scarcely half burned, which causes the enormous consumption of nearly three hundred pounds an hour. Despite all these drawbacks the speed of the "Sans Pareil" is equal at times to twenty-three miles an hour, and her average of fourteen miles an hour up to the time of being ruled out of the trial is greater than is that of the "Rocket" at the same stage of the competition.

The "Novelty," from its compact and otherwise attractive appearance, is the favorite of the public, but the engine, like the ill-fated "Sans Pareil," is a victim of imperfect construction. In the early part of the trial its water supply pipe bursts. After this is repaired one of the joints of the boiler gives away, and Ericsson has most reluctantly to withdraw from further participation in the trials. During the comparatively little time the "Novelty" is in trim her performance is really surprising. The steadiness of the engine is remarkable, even at the highest rate of speed, and in this latter respect the "Novelty" far excels either of its rivals, attaining a rate equal to forty or more miles an hour. The Liverpool *Mercury*, in summing up the results of the contest, says : "Although under the terms of the competition the directors must award the prize of £500 to the 'Rocket,' the grand prize of public opinion has already been awarded to the 'Novelty.'" However this may be, the "Rocket" is the only locomotive which, from the test of actual performance, is to be considered by the judges. Her time on the first trial is about twelve miles in forty-three minutes. In the second trial, with steam raised till it lifts the safety valve, loaded to the pressure of fifty pounds to the square inch, she draws thirteen tons weight in carriages or wagons thirty-five miles in one hour and forty-eight minutes. The average velocity attained is about twenty-nine miles an hour, or some three times that which one of

James Steam Wagon 1830

the judges had declared to be the limit of the possibilities. The experiments with the "Rocket" are performed without accident of any kind, and with no delay beyond that inseparable from the circumstances under which the contest is conducted, showing in what good stead the extensive and varied experience of the maker in railway and pit machinery has stood its designer. The "Rocket," however, brings him fame as a locomotive builder on lines which are almost as far removed from his other efforts as if he had never before constructed one. The multitubular boiler and the blast are the great essentials of his present success, and the degree to which Stephenson himself is entitled to the credit of either of these is interesting, if not, indeed, suggestive. First, as regards the boiler—it is pretty conclusive that the judges regard him as secondary, else they would not, as they have, divided the prize awarded the "Rocket," and given Booth half of it, plainly stating that they do so in recognition of his, Booth's, part in the perfection of the engine by introducing in it the multitubular boiler. Booth is the secretary of the Liverpool and Manchester Railway, and in the agitation of the question of locomotive versus fixed engine power gives much attention to the relative merits of the two. Learning of the purchase by Seguin of a Stephenson locomotive and his remodeling it, Booth slips over to France, gets an opportunity to observe what Seguin has done in adapting the American (Read's) invention of the massing of tubes for use in a locomotive boiler, and coming back to England communicates with Stephenson, and the plans of the "Rocket" are changed accordingly. So it comes about that the multitubular boiler is the "Read" in America in 1791, the "Seguin" in France in 1827, and the "Booth" in England in 1829, although as a matter of official record the American John Stevens patented a tubular boiler in England as early as 1804.

Relative to the steam blast, that Stephenson should become familiar with the plan of the "Sans Pareil" when under construction is quite natural, and that he is cognizant of what Hackworth has already done with the blast in the "Royal George" passes without question. Trevithick, Hedley and Stephenson, before Hackworth commenced experimenting, all have trouble with exhaust steam on the score of noise, and consequent endangering of life, limb and property through the frightening of horses and

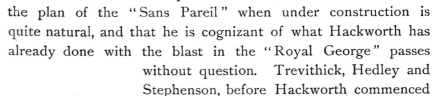

animals generally. They have all turned it into the chimney or stack to deaden the effect upon the atmosphere and lessen the popular objection to the racket on or near the public roadways. Neither of the three named, however, makes the exhaust as a means of increasing the draught a study, although it is not to be questioned that they observe it, and realize that their engines make steam faster than when the exhaust is into the open air; but they do not regard it as particularly important, if, in fact, they pay much attention to it. A good deal the same situation prevailed as regards the question of the adhesion of smooth rails until Hedley took it up, in a practical, thorough way, and demonstrated it. So it is when Hackworth grasps the solution of the exhaust steam and devises his blast pipes to get all out of this accession possible. Stephenson himself at last comprehends in a measure its importance, and in the "Rocket" improves upon the "Sans Pareil," for he hits the proportions to a nicety, whereas Hackworth's blast is so strong that it throws the blazing fuel from the chimney in perfect showers.

The effect upon the public at large of the locomotive competition is immediate, and no longer is there any talk whatever of fixed engines, ropes, and such sort of thing on the Liverpool and Manchester Railway. The shares of the company go up, and railway enterprises in all parts of the kingdom are greatly stimulated. The Liverpool and Manchester Company order a number of new locomotives

53

The Original York 1831

of Stephenson—not exactly duplicates of the "Rocket" in general principles, but nearly so. They are larger and heavier, some of them having ten and others eleven-inch cylinders, with sixteen-inch stroke and five-foot driving wheels. They have outside cylinders fixed to the fire-box, but less inclined than those of the "Rocket." The driving wheels are in front, or nearly under the chimney, which has a smoke-box added. The tubes in the boiler are only two inches in diameter, and from ninety to ninety-two in number.

A new cylinder to take the place of the cracked one is placed on the "Sans Pareil," and she is transferred to the Bolton and Leigh Railway, which has two planes—one a mile and a half long and rising seventy-three feet to the mile, and the other of about the same extent, with an elevation of a hundred and seventy-six feet to the mile. Up the first named plane the "Sans Pareil" draws a train aggregating fifteen tons at the rate of nine miles an hour; while on the steeper incline, with a weight of nearly fifteen tons, it makes a speed equal to nine to eleven miles an hour.

While thus England is interested as never before in the locomotive, America also has her sensation of a similar nature, although as a locomotive has never yet been seen or built on the continent it cannot be in the form of a contest such as that at Rainhill. Peter Cooper, a well-known merchant of New York, is America's pioneer locomotive builder, and while it is not much of a creation which he brings to Baltimore in 1829 it is something to run by steam on rails, without cogs or the like, and as such is an entire novelty. Cooper owns a very large tract of land in the city. It is situated most advantageously for manufacturing purposes, directly within the harbor, and its future, he believes, depends greatly upon the success of the Baltimore and Ohio Railroad. What the city will amount to without the company he does not care to contemplate, and does not propose to

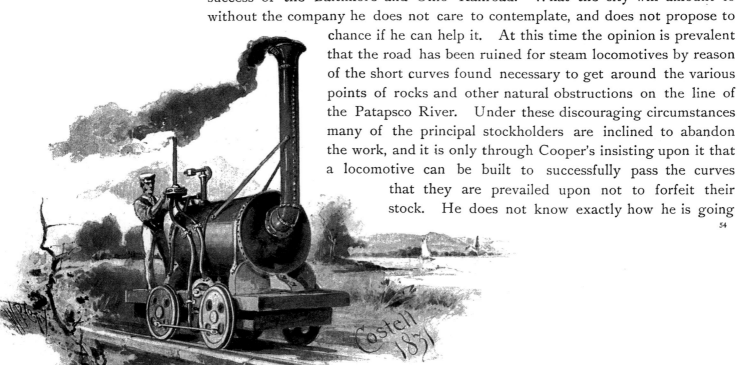

chance if he can help it. At this time the opinion is prevalent that the road has been ruined for steam locomotives by reason of the short curves found necessary to get around the various points of rocks and other natural obstructions on the line of the Patapsco River. Under these discouraging circumstances many of the principal stockholders are inclined to abandon the work, and it is only through Cooper's insisting upon it that a locomotive can be built to successfully pass the curves that they are prevailed upon not to forfeit their stock. He does not know exactly how he is going

1829 to bring this about, but with characteristic Americanism he determines it must be done. Cooper's knowledge of boilers is not very extensive, although he has done some experimenting in this line before now and has produced one or two striking results. He decides it must be an upright and tubular, but he has no tubes. This is not serious to such a man, and he buys up a lot of unmounted gun barrels from a maker in New York and substitutes them, finally completing a boiler about five feet high and less than two feet in diameter. This he brings to Baltimore and confers with Ross Winans, assistant to Chief Engineer Knight, of the Baltimore and Ohio, as to mounting it. Four wheels belonging to the company are provided, a frame made, and the thing put in shape for the first trial, which is not successful; the primitive nature of the machinery and the haste in which it has been thrown together serving to, as Cooper declares, answer well enough for a stationary engine, but such is not what he is after. He, however, does not give it up—far from it. Remaining in Baltimore some days, and unable to figure the plan out to his satisfaction, he returns to New York, thinks a good deal, and finally decides to turn the whole business over to George W. Johnson, who has a machine shop in Baltimore and is himself a mechanic of considerable ability. Among his apprentices is James Milholland, an exceedingly bright boy with a natural aptitude for machinery, and a head on his shoulders older than his years, so far as maturity of thought indicates. These two—the man Johnson and the boy Milholland—take the "Cooper" as it comes to them, and in the little shop go to work, putting the parts in condition, and following the instructions of Peter Cooper, to make the machine so that it will run no matter what it costs.

It is now about time that the locomotives ordered by Horatio Allen, in England, for the Honesdale road, should show up. They have been a long time en route. The vessel "John Jay," with the locomotive "Stourbridge Lion" on board, is at last sighted, and on the 17th of May is tied up at the wharf of the West Point Foundry Works, foot of Beach street, New York City. This means that the first real steam locomotive ever seen in America is at hand and an epoch reached of the very highest magnitude. After a short stay in New York the "Lion" is shipped up the North River to Rondout, thence by canal to Honesdale, and is immediately set up by Allen. It is mounted upon

55

four wheels, and in general appearance looks a good deal like a gigantic grass-hopper. The boiler is horizontal with a tube-shaped fire-box, branching into two short tubes at its front end and extending into a chambered smoke-box. Two vertical, double acting cylinders are secured to the outside of the boiler at the rear end with piston rods extending through the upper head to a walking beam above, the connection being at the back of the lever. The walking beam is pivoted at the extreme front end to the upper end of a swinging link, which is maintained in parallel vertical movement at the piston rod end by double links attached to either side, and secured to uprights from the cylinder head and diagonal stays to the foot of the swinging link at the forward end. A connecting rod from each walking beam attached just forward of the piston rod connection extends downward to a crank pin in each wheel. Slide valves for each cylinder are worked by eccentrics on the rear axle, the direction of the motion being changed from the horizontal to the vertical through arms on a shaft, under the frames at the back of the engine. The exhaust enters a box located under the boiler, and from there passes forward into the front of the smoke-box and upward into the stack. A pump located on the left hand side and worked from the walking beam supplies water to the boiler. The track of the Honesdale road consists of hemlock stringers or rails six by twelve inches, to which are spiked bars of rolled iron three and a quarter inches wide and one-half an inch thick. The hemlock rails are supported by caps of timber placed ten feet from center to center. The locomotive weighs seven instead of three tons, as was agreed upon when ordered. The trestles are slender and the curves sharp. Allen is begged not to trust his life to the chance of this comparatively weak structure holding up so monstrous a mass of iron, wood and steam. But Horatio is lusty, courageous and ambitious. The "Stourbridge Lion," the first locomotive on American soil, is standing on the track puffing and hissing, apparently anxious to distinguish itself. So is Allen, and to start with he moves the engine cautiously forward and back along the coal dock, and then, believing she will work, he merrily invites those about him to jump on and take a ride. They won't, not a mother's son of them, and finally Allen, determined to see what is in the "Lion," pulls the throttle valve wide open and lets her go "lickety split"

around the abrupt curve, over the swaying trestle, and out of the sight of the cheering though apprehensive crowd. Back he comes all right, but he is satisfied even with this short experience that as a railway for steam power in the shape of the locomotive the Honesdale road is not to be thought of. Next day another brief trial is made with the "Lion," and Allen's notion of the eternal fitness of things as regards a hemlock road becomes a conviction, and the "Lion" goes to the shed. Almost simultaneously with this decision another locomotive for the Honesdale road arrives in New York, the "America," the engine Allen ordered from Stephenson. But it gets no farther than the yard of Edward Dunscomb on Water street, where it is set up, its wheels raised above the ground by wooden posts and a fire kindled in the boiler. In this manner the operation of the machinery is studied, and no ordinary delight given to the crowds who come to see it in motion. The "America" is on four wheels, with a horizontal boiler, two cylinders, one on each side, set at an angle over the back wheels, which are outside and connected with the front wheels. The third engine, the "Agenoria," built by Foster & Rastrick, and in most respects the duplicate of the "Stourbridge Lion," by the same makers, remains in England.

The Mount Clare station of the Baltimore and Ohio is established in Baltimore at the extreme western end of Pratt street. It is a little box surrounded by rough sheds, and tickets are on sale for excursion trips to the Carrollton viaduct, one mile out. The car for passengers is a flat platform on four wheels, and there are no seats, the ticket holders standing together as best they can as the horse jogs along over the road. The completion of the track is being pushed with comparative rapidity. After the ground is brought to a level, square holes are dug four feet apart, twenty inches wide, two feet long and two feet deep. These holes are filled level full of broken stones securely rammed down, each particle or piece of stone having first been tested by being passed through an iron ring to insure its having the proper dimensions. After the foundation is thus made, a trench six inches deep is dug connecting each hole with the one opposite. These trenches are also filled with stones, and upon them a cedar sleeper, or cross-piece, seven feet long, is laid. These cedar cross-pieces are placed

57

The Improved York

with great care and accuracy, a spirit level being used to adjust them properly. In each end of these cross-pieces, immediately above the stone foundation, notches are cut, and into them wooden rails or stringers are carefully leveled and secured by wedges. These stringers are of yellow pine and from twenty to twenty-four feet long, six inches square, and beveled on the top of the upper side to clear the flange of the wheels, which is on the outside, not the inside, as on some lines. On top of the stringers the iron rails are carefully nailed with wrought-iron nails four inches long. This is the construction east of Vinegar Hill. West, long granite slabs are substituted for the cedar cross-pieces and yellow pine stringers. The road is practically completed from Baltimore to Vinegar Hill, a distance of seven miles. Evan Thomas finishes his sail car, the " Meteor," and the experiments with it are productive of much curiosity, and not a little excitement, particularly when a northwester is blowing, and it comes fairly flying down the track on the return to Mount Clare. It has a basket body like that of a sleigh, a mast supporting a square sail, and the four wheels are of the Winans' pattern. A horse locomotive is also put upon the Baltimore and Ohio track, the principle being the endless platform or belt working around a drum; on the shaft carrying the drum there is a gear wheel which meshes with a pinion on the axle of road wheel. This gearing gives considerable speed to the car with a moderate gait on part of the horse.

Horatio Allen has been engaged as Chief Engineer of the South Carolina road. Charleston has been in a fever of expectancy since early in the year. In February an experiment is made—one hundred and fifty feet of railway track are laid on Wentworth street, a four-wheel car procured, and upon it forty-seven bales of cotton placed. Then a mule is hitched to the car, a whip cracks, and away goes Mr. Mule with an ease that astonishes everybody. It is a revelation and develops the drawing capacity of the mule to a degree never before imagined. There are "millions in it" as the road is, in the mind's eye, completed to Augusta and operated by mule power. In April, one hundred and seventy-five feet of track, with the strap rail, is a feature of Chisholm wharf, and the market price of mules

has gone up. In June the directors authorize the commencement of the work on the line between Charleston and Hamburg; the Legislature advances $100,000 to the company as a loan; five hundred tons of rail are delivered, and before the year closes six miles of track are completed. Things are booming in Charleston at Christmas time, 1829.

1829   Ross Winans is the first to point out the advantages of coned wheels on railways, and he is the first to employ outside instead of inside journals to the axles.   William T. James, of New York, having satisfied himself that there is something in the experiments he has been making with small models of vehicles, has produced a steam carriage capable of transporting people and of making time over the streets or roadways in or near the metropolis.   It has three wheels and two six-inch cylinders.   James abandons the reciprocating in favor of the rotary cylinders in this engine.   One feature is of particular importance—that of the four fixed eccentrics, one for the forward and one for the backing motion of each cylinder.   The slide valve of one cylinder has a half-inch lap at each end and this cylinder exhausts its steam into the other.

William H. James, of London, is also making long strides toward demonstrating that all the brightest minds in steam propulsion are not confined to the circles of locomotive inventors and makers.   It is quite remarkable when the relative merits of railways and highways are considered, that the former are commonly regarded in England as suitable for the conveyance of goods only, while speed exceeding that of the average mail coach is sought chiefly in steam passenger carriages upon the turnpikes. As a matter of fact it would appear that these steam carriages in several instances, if made to run on railroads instead of turnpikes, would make faster time as a rule than any locomotive has yet recorded. Summers and Ogles' steam carriage has run on common roads near Southampton at the rate of thirty-five miles an hour, the steam pressure with a water-tube boiler being two hundred and fifty pounds to the square inch.   James' steam carriage, working under the great pressure of three hundred pounds to the square inch, has attained equally high speed.   Gurney has no less exalted a patron than the Duke of Wellington, who has his own barouche drawn by a steam wagon at Hounslow, and it is quite the thing now for the swells to go by their own steam carriages when traveling from one section to another.

On the railways matters are progressing more or less quietly as the year draws to a close. Losh has a chair for rail-joining without the aid of a pin.   Part of the base of the chair whereon the rail rests is concave, the ends of the rail being convex.   The rails are made with half-lap joints, the end of one passing the other about three inches.   The chair is of

the usual form, with upright cheeks to keep the ends of the rails together; on each of the sides of these cheeks a perpendicular cavity is cast for receiving nobs, which keep the chairs in the proper position. The distinguished gentleman of Liverpool, who, when the Liverpool and Manchester competition was announced in the papers, said that only a parcel of charlatans would have issued such a set of conditions; that it had been proved to be impossible to make an engine go ten miles an hour; but if it was ever done he would undertake to eat a stewed locomotive wheel for breakfast—has been appointed inspector of steam packets.

Things are carried forward in all divisions of the work on the Baltimore and Ohio during the Winter of 1830, and by Spring the line is ready for the formal 1830 opening to Ellicott's Mills, fourteen miles distant from Baltimore. This takes place on the 22nd day of May, and in all that the term implies, it is the first railroad in the world to be thrown open to business. The Stockton and Darlington in England is a coal road, a line originally constructed and still operated as an adjunct to mines, and while it is a fact that passengers are carried upon it, this character of traffic is entirely secondary, several firms of stage proprietors having the privilege for stated sums of money, to run coaches upon the track, but only to such an extent as will not interfere with the transport of coal and the like. The Liverpool and Manchester is the first European railroad, as the designation has come to be understood, and is so recognized by the English people, and, for that matter, by the whole of Europe; but it has not as yet been formally opened for business, and, as this must be the basis of the record, the Baltimore and Ohio is the pioneer railroad of the world, and so passes into history. Horse power is the means of propulsion. Recent experiments with Cooper's little locomotive have indicated that the changes will result in successful operation, but there is yet some work to be done, and it is not brought out. Thomas's new sail car, the "Aeolus," is in shape, however, and makes the run to Ellicott's Mills in fine style. The principal passenger car is one which has been in use for some time, as the track has been carried along. It is a little clapboard house on four wheels, the entrance being by a step at the rear. There are two windows on each side extending the length of the car, and there is a board table

"Samson" 1831.

1830 between them upon which to deposit bundles, etc.   The driver has a seat upon
the top of this conveyance, which is drawn by a single horse.   The succeeding
day the car "Pioneer" is ready, and it is a decided improvement upon the former
equipment, inasmuch as it is open on all sides, with the rear seat facing the front,
and there is some little effort made at upholstering.   There is a roof and seats
upon it as well and on the whole the car is quite presentable.   It heads the procession on a memorable trip to the Mills, Charles Carrollton, of Carrollton, being
among the passengers.   The next morning the Baltimore *American* contains the
company's advertisement, to the effect that a brigade of cars will run three times
a day each way, from Baltimore to Ellicott's Mills, passage twenty-five cents.
Within a few weeks a more extended advertisement is inserted in the *American*,
and it is the first regular railroad time-table appearing in a newspaper in
America.   At the same time the company issues the first set of rules and
regulations to employes.

About seven and a quarter miles of the single track of the road are laid
on yellow pine stringers, and the remaining six and three-quarters on granite
or stone sleepers.   The same character of rail—that is, the flat strips of iron
known as the strap, or "snake head"—as that laid upon the stone sill portion
of the line, is now put down on the other or wooden sill division.   This has
led to a complete change in the car wheels, the flange being now upon the
inside of the wheel instead of on the outside, as formerly.   It is found that
since the change the wheels are not so liable to leave the track, and also that the
friction is lessened.   People are in Baltimore from many parts of the world to see
the operation of the Baltimore and Ohio, and reports are forwarded abroad,
which cannot do other than attract much attention.   Baron Krudener, Envoy of
the Czar of Russia, has had a ride on the Thomas sailing car, managing the sail
himself.   He declares he never enjoyed traveling so much, and it is his
announced intention to send his suite from Washington to have a sail on the
railroad.   A new passenger car made by Imlay, which has just
been put into service on the road, is far ahead of anything
yet seen.   The arrangement for the accommodation of passengers is in some respects
different from any other which has been
adopted.   The body of the carriage accom-
modates twelve persons, and the outside seats
at either end six, including the driver,

61

Jervis Experiment 1832

while on the top of the carriage, running lengthwise, there is a double sofa, which will accommodate twelve more. A wire netting rises from two sides of the top of the carriage to a height which renders the upper seats perfectly secure. The whole is surmounted by an iron frame work, with an awning to protect the passengers from the sun or rain. The carriage is named the "Ohio," and is very handsomely finished throughout.

The car for the trial trip of the "Tom Thumb," as Cooper's locomotive has been christened, is the first run on the road, and resembles an open boat, being light, and of such form as to permit everybody to see the locomotive in operation, or to jump out should the situation at any time during the journey appear to make this a wise proceeding. The "Thumb" is all ready on the 28th of August, 1830, and is to test a most important principle—that is, whether steam power can be used successfully on a line where the curvatures are of four hundred feet radius. The prevailing opinion in England is that locomotives can neither ascend heavy grades or turn very sharp curves, and this opinion is shared by some distinguished American engineers to such an extent that they believe the Baltimore and Ohio is, with its existing construction, entirely excluded from the use of locomotives. The little engine has a vertical multitubular boiler, and is mounted upon four wheels of the Winans' patent. There is one vertical, double-acting cylinder, three and one-quarter inches in diameter, and having a stroke of fourteen inches, with the piston rod passing through the upper cylinder head to a cross-head running on two round guides. The connecting rod is attached to the outer end of the cross-head and extends downward to a crank arm on an intermediate shaft secured below the frame. The end opposite to that carrying the crank arm has a gear, which meshes with another, one-half its diameter, the latter being fixed on to one of the main axles. A fan blower for maintaining a good draft is located on the platform and driven from a pulley on one of the main axles. The valves are worked by eccentrics having V hooks, giving both a forward and backward motion, controlled by hand. The supply of water for the boiler is carried in a barrel located on the platform and connected to a

The South Carolina 1832

1830 pump worked from the engine.   The exhaust is into the atmosphere.   Upon the platform of the locomotive steps Peter Cooper and with him George Brown, the Treasurer of the Baltimore and Ohio Company; Philip Thomas, its President, and a few others.   The little car containing directors and their friends, to the number of about two dozen, is attached, and Cooper, with his own hand, opens the throttle.   As the steam is admitted into the cylinder, the gear wheels revolve with a clacking noise, and the first locomotive ever built on the American continent moves off with the first load of passengers ever drawn by steam on rails in the Western hemisphere.   It runs the entire distance to Ellicott's Mills, without a break, in an hour and a quarter, and accomplishes the return trip in fifty-seven minutes.   On the way back there is a race with a horse-power car and it makes things right lively for a time, but Mr. Cooper hurts his hand in the attempt to keep the rope gearing in place, the steam is shut off, and the horse gallops ahead more frightened than ever.   The result of this trip is to set the engineers, who said that a locomotive could not be made to pass over sharp curves, by the ears, and to create an interest in steam propulsion which extends the world over.   That a little machine, weighing scarcely a ton, and having but little over one horse-power, can draw four and a half tons weight over such a line as the Baltimore and Ohio, with its grades and its curves, at an average speed exceeding twelve miles an hour, is amazing, and the more it is pondered over the greater are the congratulations that a typical American has, by the sheer force of a will acknowledging no precedent to govern where necessity compels an advance, accomplished that which both at home and abroad had been declared an impossibility.   To the Baltimore and Ohio it means everything, for with steam power and its consequent decrease of operating expenses, coupled with an increase of efficiency beyond computation, its future is made certain.   To the country as a whole it is the demonstration of an essential in railroad progress of wider and more vital importance than anything previously known in its material history.   Ross Winans declares that as between the " Rocket " and its record at the Liverpool and Manchester competition, and the " Tom Thumb " and its performance, in

B&O "Atlantic" 1832

rounding the shortest curves at a speed of from fifteen to eighteen miles an hour, and ascending grades of nearly twenty feet to the mile with scarcely a diminution of speed, the superiority of the "Tom Thumb" is very strongly apparent, especially as the "Rocket" weighs six times as much as the "Thumb" and had a track perfectly straight and level and of less than two miles length to work upon.

With matters thus progressing so favorably on the pioneer American road, its contemporary, as it were, the Charleston and Hamburg, is up and doing, and not only have its directors determined from its very inception to operate with steam power, but the first locomotive built in America for actual service on a railroad has been ordered, and by the summer of 1830 is completed at the West Point Foundry, near New York. Edward L. Miller, of Charleston, South Carolina, planned the "Best Friend," as the locomotive is named, and Charles E. Detmole made the drawings. It is a four wheel engine, with side rods. Its boiler is of the vertical multitubular type, and is carried between the axles. There are two double acting cylinders placed forward, and connected to a double crank axle which carries the rear drivers. The cylinders are on an incline to allow the cross-heads and guides to clear the front axle, and the valves are worked by one eccentric on the crank axle. The eccentric rod is connected to the lower end of a rock shaft, the upper end of which is coupled to the valve rod. A pump supplies the boiler with water. While the "Best Friend" is en route by the ship Niagara from New York to Charleston, various experiments are being made on the road as far as completed. Among others, a cranky car is obtained and upon it several bales of cotton and about a dozen people are piled, a sail car is attached, which, with a large, square sail, in a stiff breeze, whirls the load along in a lively manner. Subsequently a premium of $500 is offered by the company for the best horse locomotive, and this is awarded to Detmole for his "Flying Dutchman." This machine is built upon an endless chain platform, and when placed upon the road carries twelve passengers at the rate of twelve miles an hour. Later on the "Best Friend" arrives, is set up by David Matthews, and by running at the rate of from sixteen to twenty-one miles an hour, with forty to fifty passengers on four or five cars, or thirty to thirty-five miles an hour without cars, proves her power and efficiency to be double that contracted for. A second engine, the "Native," is built and put upon the road. She is designed and constructed by Thomas Dotterer, and has outside cylinders and straight axles.

64

1830   On the 12th of August, 1830, the Mohawk and Hudson Railroad in New York, to connect the cities of Albany and Schenectady, little less than sixteen miles apart, is commenced.   John B. Jervis is the chief engineer.   The Schuylkill Railroad in Pennsylvania, extending from Port Carbon some ten miles to the vicinity of the town of Tuscarora, and intended exclusively for coal, is finished. There are two sets of tracks, each of only twenty inches gauge.   The construction is of white oak with iron rails an inch and a half wide, and three-eighths of an inch thick at the center, the upper surface being convex.

The 15th of September, 1830, is a great day in the history of the railway in England; the greatest in her annals of progress to this time.   It is the opening of the Liverpool and Manchester, designated by eminent engineers and scientists "The Grand British Experimental Railway."   The stupendous work is inaugurated with countless numbers of people assembled at Liverpool to witness the show, ceremony, procession and festivity provided for the occasion.   Eight locomotives constructed by the Stephensons are put into requisition for the purpose.   The Duke of Wellington, Prime Minister; Sir Robert Peel, Secretary of State, and other high dignitaries are present, and it is truly a most memorable event.

The succeeding day the railway is open for business.   Of thirty-one miles of track, eighteen are laid with stone blocks and thirteen with wooden sleepers or larch, the latter being put down principally across the embankment and the two districts of the Moss.   The rails are of wrought-iron divided into fish-bellied sections, each section being supported by a cast-iron chair, to which it is secured by a wooden wedge.   The cars for carrying passengers are without roofs, the body consisting of four sills, and side and end framing being boarded up. There are no springs, and the journal boxes are bolted to the sills.   The burden cars are simply platforms on wheels, with canvas covers tied down over such merchandise as might be damaged by sparks or inclement weather.   The coal car is the black wagon or chaldron, holding between three to four tons.   The Duke of Wellington has a special coach built for himself, which has a roof and can be made private with curtains at the sides.   The cost of the Liverpool and Manchester has reached nearly £800,000, or something like £25,000, or $125,000 per mile.   The

The James
1832

month following the opening of the line Stephenson finishes and places in service the "Planet," which is a striking improvement upon all his previous efforts. In it he adopts the arrangement of cylinders and driving axles designed by Hackworth in the "Globe," the latter named engine designed by Hackworth and built by the Stephensons for the Stockton and Darlington road not having as yet been delivered. The "Planet" is the first inside cylinder engine made by Stephenson, and in it he presents the first combination of horizontal cylinders and crank axle with the multitubular boiler. The cylinders are, furthermore, encased in the smoke-box, and this is kept hot by the heat escaping from the tubes, an arrangement suggested to Stephenson by Trevithick. The "Planet" weighs nine tons and has drawn a train of seventy-six tons at the rate of fifteen and a half miles an hour. Her cylinders are eleven inches in diameter with a stroke of sixteen inches, driving wheels five feet and leading wheels three feet in diameter. In the "Mercury," which immediately follows the "Planet," and is of the same type, with the improvement of raising the frame so as to be above the driving axle, George Stephenson reaches the highest state of his development, the "Mercury" being regarded as the standard pattern of the English four-wheel locomotive.

No single man to this time has contributed more to the establishment of the railway than George Stephenson. He has advocated its advantages upon every occasion, and shown that he has comprehended transport by rail as no one else has done. In the positions gained by the sheer force of his indomitable will, he has been largely instrumental in compelling the consideration of the locomotive; but there is no record established by him to prove that he is the inventor of any essential part of the locomotive engine. Further, it is difficult to say in what respect he has actually improved its structure or working otherwise than by adopting and successfully executing the plans and suggestions of others. Indeed, upon his ability to quickly distinguish genuine improvements, and his capacity to make application of them in construction, must rest his achievements. His earlier projects relative to the locomotive have been without practical value, and there is no essential which owes its origin to him. On the other hand, Timothy Hackworth is original, is actually of himself improving the locomotive in essentials as no other man is doing, and is

B & O "Traveller" 1852

incomparably in advance of George Stephenson in everything which may be truly said to lay claim to distinction. He has and is stamping a character upon the structure of the locomotive of the very highest importance, judging from the practical results following his efforts. In the "Globe," the new passenger engine, which he has placed upon the Stockton and Darlington road, he is the first to secure steadiness at a high speed through horizontal cylinders and a crank driving axle. The boiler is of the single flue type, the fire-box being placed in the flue, in the front end of which a number of water tubes are fixed diametrically across, and in such a way as to deflect the products of combustion into a spiral course. An entirely original feature, a copper steam dome, is fixed upon the boiler, and from this the engine receives its name. The four coupled wheels are five feet in diameter. The driving axle has two cranks set at right angles. The cylinders are horizontal and side by side, while the two eccentrics are loose on the driving axle, and may be reversed by a single lever. The "Globe" has demonstrated a speed equal to fifty miles an hour, and is undoubtedly one of the fastest engines in the world. In the "Middlesboro," for freight or goods purposes, Hackworth introduces for the first time six wheels, three pairs coupled. The engine has inside frames, and requires a tender at each end. There are no lathes large enough to turn off wheels when keyed on the axle, and, therefore, Hackworth makes his wheels of cast-iron in two portions—a large central boss and an annular rim. The latter is fastened to the former by oak tree-nails, through which iron bolts or wedges are driven at intervals to insure greater tightness. The tires of wrought-iron are shrunk upon the outer cast-iron rim, which can be readily removed from or placed upon the central boss.

There are, in this good year of 1830, no less than three types of horizontal-cylinder engines with crank axles—the "Bury," Stephenson's "Planet" and Hackworth's "Globe." James Kennedy is the designer of the "Bury" engine, which has inside frames, as have all the Stockton and Darlington engines, she having been built for that line. The engine, which is round-backed, and has a dome-topped fire-box, is the best yet constructed. The character of the frames and all the working parts is exceptionally good, and indicates a progress most commendable. She also has the largest driv-

Stephenson's "Patentee" 1833

ing wheels introduced up to this time; they are six feet in diameter, and the speed attained, now that a multitubular boiler has been fitted, is reported at the high rate of fifty-eight miles an hour on a level and with a load of twelve wagons. If this is true—and it appears well authenticated—Bury will make Hackworth look to his laurels. Bury's first engine on six wheels, the "Dreadnought," is found to be too heavy for the Stockton and Darlington track.

Losh has introduced wheels with wrought-iron spokes and rim, and they are largely taking the place of those with cast-iron rims hooped with wrought-iron. The wheel Stephenson adopted on the Liverpool and Manchester has cast-iron naves and wooden spokes, and rims on which wrought-iron tires are laid. Square boxes are cast in the nave to receive one end of the spokes, the other end being inserted in the fellies in the same manner as in coach wheels. A thin wrought-iron rim is laid around the fellies and upon this the outside or flanged tire is placed.

In the "Swift," built by Hawthorne for the Stockton and Darlington, the intermediate shaft and peculiar eccentrics used cause no little remark. Captain John Ericsson and Charles Vignoles have a plan for using a middle rail on steep inclines and for a pair of wheels on vertical axles, which shall grip the rail on each side. The idea is that these wheels will give sufficient power to carry a train where the ordinary driving wheels of an engine would slip. The Stockton and Darlington people report the saving effected by the use of locomotives over horses is only about a third, a most significant statement when taking into consideration that the cost of coal to them is hardly a twentieth part of what it is in some sections of the kingdom.

Steam carriages continue to multiply. Rowe & Boase propose a multitubular boiler with each tube bent into a spiral figure of three turns. Hanson has the wheels on his machine so arranged that they roll in an inclined position as well as parallel, and thus get around curves easier. Heaton has a most perplexing combination of gearing; Summer and Ogle and Hancock come out with improved carriages. Brown builds an immense carriage, moved by gas vacuum. Gillet has a scheme for what he terms a perpetual railway; and in the interest of his compressed air coach Mann issues a book, in which his calculations show a requirement of two thousand cubic feet of the

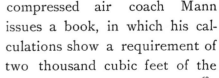

1830 natural density to propel a carriage weighing, with its load, two tons, at the rate of fourteen miles an hour. It is difficult to believe there is really nothing new under the sun in the light of the multiplicity of invention in the single direction of steam propulsion on land.

In the United States William T. James, of New York, builds a full-size steam carriage to run on the public highway. This, his fourth creation, has three wheels, the rear pair being the drivers, three feet in diameter, and the third is the front, or steering wheel. There are double cylinders five inches in diameter, with a ten-inch stroke, placed horizontally, and the valves are operated by four eccentrics.

The imperfections of the snake-head rails in the United States, as well as the English substitutes, which have come into use, have led an American, Robert L. Stevens, of Hoboken, son of Col. John Stevens of extended railroad fame, to devise an improvement which at once gains favor. The rail best known, and adopted by most of the English roads, and used to considerable extent in America, is without a base, and requires, owing to its peculiar shape, a chair on each cross-tie or stone block, as the case may be. Stevens, on his voyage to Europe to order an English engine for the Camden and Amboy road, spent a good deal of his time, Yankee fashion, whittling with a jack-knife, the incentive to this proceeding being a desire to get up a better style of rail than those in use. So he kept on consuming soft pine until he had completed the model of a cross section to his liking. Reaching home he has his plans so matured that the H rail, as he terms it, materializes, and is now being made in considerable quantities. It is a rail which can be spiked with hook-headed spikes direct to the bearing, and has iron tongues which are attached to the rail by rivets put on hot. The rail weighs forty-two pounds to the yard, is three and a half inches high, the width of the head is two and a half inches, and the base three and a half inches.

Colonel Stephen H. Long, of the United States Topographical Engineers, and with Jonathan Knight, the original engineer of the Baltimore and Ohio road, has obtained a charter from the State of Pennsylvania, incorporating the "American Steam Carriage Company," and, locating in Philadelphia, he is now at work on the construction of a locomotive. In design it is much after the order of the improved English type, but it has some original points.

In Baltimore the remodeling of the "Cooper" locomotive, at the shop of George W. Johnson, and the success met with when the little engine is put on the road, has led Johnson and his assistant, Milholland, to the belief that together they can devise and build a locomotive without in any respect infringing upon Cooper's idea. So they keep quietly at work until the end of the year, with the result that they have a locomotive finished and are awaiting an opportunity to demonstrate its abilities on the Baltimore and Ohio tracks. The engine has four wheels, one pair being drivers. There are two vertical, double-acting cylinders located on the back bumper. The cross-heads are above the cylinders and the connecting rods extend from them up to the back ends of walking beams. The opposite or front ends of the beams have rods reaching down to crank arms on the end of a shaft carried on the frame. At the center of the shaft there is a gear which engages with another one on the axle of the road wheel. The boiler is horizontal, with twin fire-boxes at the back end, the first time such have been introduced in locomotive construction. Three flues run from the top of each fire-box to the smoke-box at the front end of the boiler. The cylinders have steam chests on their front sides, and the valves are driven from the walking beam. The valve rod from the beam has a double V end which engages with either one of two pins on an arm fulcrumed between the pins, which give opposite motions. The motion is carried to the valve through a right-angled arm connection to a bell crank. No pump is provided, the boiler being filled through the safety valve. The exhaust is through a central vertical pipe at the back of the boiler.

There is not a long wait for an opportunity to get the "Johnson" under steam, as coincident with the new year an advertisement appears in the Baltimore papers telling of the company's determination to pay substantially for such product of American brain and ingenuity as represented in a type of locomotive which will answer the demands of the pioneer railroad. In other words, the announcement which heads the editorial page of the *American* on January 5th, 1831, is to the 1831 effect that the Baltimore and Ohio Railroad Company, being desirous of obtaining a supply of locomotive engines of American manufacture adapted to its road, will pay the sum of $4,000 for the most approved engine which shall be delivered for trial on or before the 1st of June, 1831; and will also pay $3,500 for the next best. The engine must burn coke or coal and consume its own smoke; must

1831 not when in operation weigh more than three and a half tons, and on a level
road must be capable of drawing day by day fifteen tons weight, inclusive of the
weight of the wagons, at a speed of fifteen miles an hour. The company is to furnish
wagons or cars of Winans' construction, the friction of which will not exceed five
pounds to the ton. The preference in adjudging the relative advantages, all
things being equal, will be given to the engine weighing the least. The flanges
are to run on the inside of the rails. The pressure of steam must not exceed
one hundred pounds to the square inch, and there must be two safety valves,
neither of them fastened down. The engine and boiler must be supported on
springs and carried on four wheels. There must be a mercurial gauge to show the
steam pressure above fifty pounds, and constructed to blow off at one hundred
and twenty pounds. The test is to be thirty days' regular work upon the road,
and it can commence at any time. The company offers to furnish the tender and
the supply of water and fuel. This, the first proposal in the United States for
locomotives, is followed by the expressed willingness of the Company to furnish
its standard wheels to the contestants if desired, and to extend every possible
facility in expediting construction. The first to appear on the road in response to
the offer is the "Johnson"; the next is the "York," designed by Phineas Davis,
and built by him and his partner Gardner, in the town in Pennsylvania from which
the engine takes its name. Davis is by profession a watchmaker, but has for
some time had a machine shop with Gardner, the two giving a great deal of
attention to machinery calculated to be adaptable for locomotives. Davis is a
natural mechanic of considerable originality, but without in any large degree the
actual experience in steam working machinery requisite to a thorough carrying
out of his ideas. His will is strong and his purpose defined in his
own mind and in the production he accomplishes, after a fashion which
tells strongly in his favor. The "York" has all four wheels coupled,
and the boiler is of the multitubular type and vertical
or bottle-shaped. There are two double-acting
cylinders placed on the outside of the boiler; the
piston rods extend through the lower heads and
connect to the cross-heads with rods running
down vertically and connected to the center of
trussed parallel rods, reaching from wheel to
wheel and connected to crank pins in the wheels.
The valves are worked by cams on the axle of

71

one of the road wheels. There are two cams for each cylinder with one
shifting yoke operated by foot pressure for front and back motion. The pump
to supply the boiler is worked from the cross-head and the steam exhausts into
the open air. The third locomotive is from Philadelphia, and named the
"Costell," designed and built by Stacey Costell, a man of much inventive ability,
who has, among other things perfected a vibrating steam engine, which has met
with a good deal of favor. He has organized the Penn Locomotive and Engine
Company, and the locomotive now on the Baltimore and Ohio tracks is the first
effort of this company. The boiler is a horizontal one, after the Galloway
pattern, having an internal horizontal fire tube pierced by several vertical water
tubes. The fire door is at one end of the boiler and the smoke stack at the other.
There are two double-acting, oscillating cylinders, placed on the frames under the
boiler, the piston rod extending through both heads with one end coupled direct to
a crank arm on a short cross-shaft. Each end of the shaft has a crank arm, set
quartering, and a spur gear at its center engaging a smaller one or one of the
road-wheel shafts. Mounted at the fire-door end of the boiler and above it is a
four-way valve with two pipes running to each cylinder. Two hollow rings are
placed against the cylinder and receive the pipes from the four-way valve, the
rings being parted at the center with ports at each parting into each end of the
cylinder. The four-way valve is connected by a pipe to the boiler, and by turning
its handle one pipe admits steam to the cylinder while its opposite conveys the
steam through the four-way valve to the atmosphere. By changing the handle
forty-five degrees the functions of the pipes are changed and the engine is
reversed. A pump supplies water to the boiler and all four wheels of the locomotive are coupled.

The fourth aspirant for the Baltimore and Ohio prize is another watchmaker,
Ezekiel Child, also a Philadelphian of varied talents, an inventive genius, of
persistent application and as original as energetic. His engine, like that of his
townsman, Costell, is upon four wheels, all coupled, but his boiler is vertical,
multitubular, and set midway between the four
wheels. One rotary cylinder is set forward of the
boiler on the frame. The cylinder has two sliding
abutments, operated by two cams
secured to the shaft of the rotary
cylinder. Four valves, two admission
and two exhaust, on each end of the

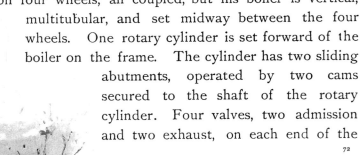

The Campbell 1836

1831 cylinder are operated by an arm attached to and revolving with the cylinder shaft. The shifting of the arm on the shaft changes the functions of the valve from admission to exhaust and reverses the engine, the operation being controlled by a lever in the hands of the engineer. Steam is admitted to the cylinder through its central shaft at one end, and exhausted at the opposite end into the atmosphere.

The fifth and last locomotive entered in the competition is that of William T. James, of New York. This is his fifth effort in construction for steam propulsion on land, but his first to run on rails. It has James' distinctive boiler, vertical, and with fire-box surrounded with a water space, but without tubes. There are four wheels, all coupled, and at the center of the frame carrying the wheels an upright wooden frame is constructed. Two double-acting vertical cylinders are placed upon the horizontal platform, with piston rods extending through their upper heads, connected to cross-heads running upon guides, and with connecting rods coupled at their upper ends to cranks on a shaft supported above the cylinders on the upright wooden frame, the cranks being at each end set quartering, and having two different-sized gears near their centers, also two eccentrics for each steam valve. Above the shaft mentioned is another, parallel to the first one, but long enough to extend beyond the upright frames, and have at each outer end a crank arm set quartering, and at its center, or nearly so, two different-sized gears—a large one, to run into the small one on the first shaft, and a small one, to run into the large one on the second shaft, the object being to change the speed and power of the second shaft. They run on a spline and are shifted by hand. To the outer crank arms of the second shaft, at each end, is attached a combination of three rods made in a triangle, the two lower corners being attached to the rod wheels, one to each, the two angular rods forming main rods to each wheel, and the horizontal rod forming the coupling or parallel rod. The valves are worked by two eccentrics, each attached to a curved connecting piece for sure reversing. The exhaust is into the stack.

A most striking feature of this quintette of locomotives is their originality, no one being like another, and not one of the five copying European practice in the slightest. American independence of thought

73

and an equally characteristic boldness in conception and consummation marks every step of the way to locomotive power on the Baltimore and Ohio. Other American railroads have received or have ordered foreign locomotives, in the belief that the American comprehension of the requirements and the ability to meet them are not equal to the occasion; but the Baltimore and Ohio is most essentially and pre-eminently an American road, and as such has nothing whatever in common with other American companies which are actuated by the fallacy that American genius is not equal to the situation. If there is to be a distinctive type of locomotives owing its origin and development to American brains, the Baltimore and Ohio marks its foundation in the competition of 1831, with the first aggregation of motive power to any extent on the American continent, and all of it characteristically American.

One after another the five locomotives are tested, and finally the palm of superiority is awarded Phineas Davis' "York," and the $4,000 paid the sturdy and indomitable watchmaker of the Pennsylvania town, with the understanding that his engine is to be changed considerably and on the lines proposed by Ross Winans, the Company's Assistant of Machinery. It is also agreed that Davis shall remain identified with the Baltimore and Ohio to the extent of the perfection of the plans and the construction in his own shops of a number of locomotives for service on the road. An arrangement is entered into with Child to leave his engine on the line for switching and yard use, and another with James, looking to further experimenting with his locomotive. The "Costell" is taken back to Philadelphia for certain changes and trials there, while the "Johnson" goes to the place of its maker to serve as the basis of various experiments by James Millholland, now the foreman of the shop, and who has determined to go thoroughly into the details of application and construction.

Lafayette 1837

Meanwhile, Winans and Davis have been going over the matter of the changes in the "York" with a view to simplifying and bettering its working, so that when the engine again appears upon the road it will serve as the standard for others to the number the company may decide upon. Davis sends to his shop at York for the shingles and scraps of boards upon which he made the original drawings of the locomotive, and finally the remodeled "York" is on the track ready for service. It is still upon four wheels and the boiler remains vertical, but in it has been adapted the plan of tube arrangement and general style of the boiler of the Cooper engine, which developed such good steam-making qualities on its original trial and the patent right of which Davis has bought from Cooper.   The cylinders, two in number, are double-acting, and placed in front of the boiler each side of the center at a little angle, the piston rod extending out through the lower head and attached to a cross-head.   The connecting rod from the cross-head takes hold at its lower end of a crank arm on the end of a shaft fastened to the framing.   The crank arms on the two ends being set quartering.   On the center of the shaft is a gear running into another on the axle of one pair of road wheels, which become drivers.   The valves are worked by cams, each valve having a go-ahead and a backing cam, with a yoke to go over them, shifted by foot pressure according to the direction it is desired to move the engine.   A pump is driven by the cross-head to supply water to the boiler.   The exhaust drives a fan which blows the fire.   The road wheels run in Winans' frictionless bearings.   The "York" thus becomes the pioneer engine in actual service on the Baltimore and Ohio, and demonstrates a capacity of running at a speed of thirteen to fourteen miles an hour with an aggregate load of fourteen tons.   It burns anthracite coal and weighs three and a half tons.   The curvatures of the road are all traveled by it with great facility, and on straight sections the locomotive with its cars has reached a speed of thirty miles an hour, while it frequently makes twenty miles an hour, and fifteen or more on curves of four hundred feet radius.   It is a thoroughly practical locomotive, the realization of Peter Cooper's hopes, and in making the "York" what it now is too much credit cannot be given to Ross Winans for the part he has had in thus perfecting what is undoubtedly the most practical and thoroughly good engine for the purposes for which it has been constructed at this day in the United States.

The West Point Foundry has finished its second locomotive for the South Carolina Railroad, and it is now in service on that line, thanks to the indomitable push and energy of Horatio Allen.   This engine is named the "West Point," and as designed by Allen, who is the Chief

Hercules
1837

Engineer of the Company, has the same size frame, wheels and cranks as the "Best Friend," but a horizontal instead of an upright boiler, with iron tubes two and a half inches in diameter and about six feet long. In other respects the "West Point" is practically a duplication of the "Best Friend," but is proving a better engine in many ways. The South Carolina road is constructed very largely on wooden piles and trestles, as substitutes for both sleepers and embankments. The superstructure is of flat bars attached to wooden stringers, six by nineteen inches, supported on piles which are secured by ties. The piles are driven in some of the marshes to a great depth, and in other places they are used instead of " fills." Early in the year the " Best Friend," all cleaned and oiled up especially for the occasion, is attached to two cars—one filled with people and the other with a detachment of United States troops and a field piece—and amid the booming of cannon and the shouts of the multitude, the first anniversary of the commencement of the road is celebrated. Some time later the " Best Friend" explodes her boiler. Her negro fireman, not being satisfied with the ordinary slow progress of getting up steam, fastens the safety valve down, with the result that when the next census is taken of the colored population of South Carolina that darky had not yet reached terra firma on his return trip. The wreck of the " Best Friend " is taken in hand by Thomas Dotterer, who, in rebuilding it, substitutes straight axles, cast wheels and wrought tires for the former crank axles, wooden wheels and iron tires. Quite appropriately her name is changed to the " Phœnix."

The Mohawk and Hudson Railroad is completed, and the engine built for it at the West Point Foundry on the order of John B. Jervis, and named the "De Witt Clinton," is finished, and history records the running of the first locomotive in the State of New York. It is the ninth day of August, 1831, and a large and curious throng of people, most of them decidedly skeptical, have congregated at the old tavern about a mile out from Albany to witness the proceedings. There stands the "fiery monster," as the "Clinton" looks to be to many, and behind her the stage-coach-looking cars, each upon four wheels fitted to the track, and a brake to keep them there if found necessary. The "De Witt Clinton" has two cylinders, five and a half inches in diameter, and with a sixteen-inch stroke. There are four wheels, all drivers, with wrought-iron tires.

The cranks are inside, and there are outside connecting rods. The boiler is tubular, with drop furnace, two fire-doors, one above the other, and copper tubes two and a half inches in diameter and six feet long. The cylinders are on an incline, and two vertical pumps for supplying the boiler with water are driven by a bell crank. The engine weighs three and a half tons. The trial trip, which is the first on the continent on any such extensive scale as a whole train of cars, is not exactly a picnic for the passengers, although they all declare it great. The car, or coach trucks, are coupled together, with chains or chain links, leaving from two to three feet slack. As the locomotive starts and the slack is taken up, those on the front seats pitch headforemost against those on the back seats, and as the train comes to a sudden stop those on the back seats return the compliment. The dry pitch pine fuel, as it is consumed in the engine, pours out great volumes of black smoke, thickly impregnated with cinders and sparks, and the umbrellas so quickly raised as a protection soon disappear, the alpaca or silk simply adding to the destruction of the occasion, which spares nothing that is inflammable. The consequence is that each good passenger helps the other, who, like himself, is so luckless as to have an outside seat, and the constant slapping of one and another's garments to retain at the least a semblance of habiliment suggests a jollity and freedom of personal intercourse which is in reality by no means what it may seem at a distance. The performance of the locomotive notwithstanding gives the highest satisfaction from a railroad point of view, for the "Clinton" shows at times a speed of thirty miles an hour, and makes the run in less than an hour, including stoppages. Soon after this an English locomotive, built by Stephenson and named the "Robert Fulton," arrives in this country, and is placed upon the Mohawk and Hudson. It is double the weight of the "Clinton," being of the "Planet" type, and proves too heavy for the line, injuring the track to such an extent that it is not generally used. The rails are of strap iron laid on yellow pine stringers, a flange being provided to give the iron an increased stiffness and to hold it more firmly to the stringer. The straps are nearly three-quarters of an inch thick and two and a half inches wide, while the stringers are six inches square. Over the embankments the rail is

supported by cedar cross-ties, on which cast-iron chairs are fastened to receive 1831 the stringers, which are secured by a key or wedge. In excavations the stringers rest on stone blocks, secured in the same way by cast-iron chairs. Later a second English engine is received on the Mohawk and Hudson, and named the "John Bull." It is of Stephenson's make, with the characteristics of the "Samson" and "Goliath," two locomotives he has still under construction at the works at Newcastle. The "Bull," like the "Fulton," is much too heavy for the road, although used to a greater or less extent, as occasion demands.

Much trouble is experienced with the rigidity of the frames of these large English engines, and their passing around the curves on the line is always attended with difficulty. Jervis is experimenting with them, trying to devise some way of more equally distributing the weight, and thus avoid the severe vertical motion experienced whenever passing over inequalities in the track. A like difficulty is being experienced with the "Herald," an English locomotive, built by Stephenson, and imported by the Baltimore and Susquehanna Railroad, which is now completed for a distance of nearly seven miles east of Baltimore. The "Herald," owing to its rigidity and large wheels, is continually getting off the track. Ross Winans is devising a plan to obviate this by taking off the front wheels and substituting other and smaller ones.

There is a second English engine, named the "John Bull," on the Camden and Amboy Railroad, and it, too, is of Stephenson build, being of the "Planet" type. It arrived at Bordentown, N. J., in August and has inside cylinders connected direct to the driving wheels and a multitubular boiler. The driving wheels have cast-iron hubs and locust wood spokes and fellies, with tires five inches wide, flanged and shrunk on like the tire of an ordinary wagon wheel. The steam pipes are inside the boiler and the dome over the fire-box, and in the dome is a lock on the safety valve which the engineer cannot reach. On the day of the trial trip, in November, there being nothing sent with the engine in the shape of a tender, a whiskey barrel is placed on a flat car, a leather hose made by a shoemaker, and attached by wax thread, is connected from the barrel to the boiler, and in this way the water is supplied. The "Bull" weighs ten tons, and is the largest locomotive yet imported from England and the heaviest at this time anywhere in the country. Too large, in fact, to be handled satisfactorily on the Camden and

Amboy in its present shape, notwithstanding the fact that it is laid with the Stevens rail, which is considered the best now in existence for heavy traffic. The cars drawn by the "Bull" are somewhat similar in appearance to those used on the Mohawk and Hudson, but finer and better in every way. Despite the fact that so many foreign engines are being imported by the different lines, horse power is still largely used by the Mohawk and Hudson, the Camden and Amboy and the Philadelphia and Columbia, particularly for passenger service. The English engines do not give general satisfaction, being apparently of faulty construction, and requiring almost incessant repair or alteration. They do not appear to be adapted for American lines.

Two miles of the Newcastle and Frenchtown railroad in Pennsylvania are completed by July 4th, and on that day the first locomotive built by Colonel Long is given a trial. It is not a success, failing to generate sufficient steam to propel it more than a short distance. Next day the Colonel tries it again with better results, as he succeeds in covering the two miles, but only this and nothing more. Off and on during the summer Long experiments with this engine on the Frenchtown road, and, failing to demonstrate any reasonable efficiency in it, finally withdraws it altogether—a wiser man, he says, than ever before as to the requirements of a successful locomotive.

The first eight-wheel passenger car to run on any railroad in the world is placed upon the Baltimore and Ohio Railroad on July 4th, in fitting commemoration of the nation's anniversary, and named the "Columbus." It was built in the company's shops, from the drawings of Ross Winans and under his personal supervision. The "Columbus" has a body double the length of the ordinary four-wheeled cars, and is placed upon two four-wheeled trucks, with Winans' friction wheels. The car has no springs, and the passengers' baggage is carried on top. The motive power is operated by means of a perch attached to the running gear. The body of the car is attached to each truck by a bolster and center bolt, about which the truck turns or swivels. Experience with the "Columbus," as well as other cars in the service, leads Jonathan Knight, the Chief Engineer, to make a report to the company, strongly recommending the use

Hinkley's "Lion" 1859

of springs on every car in use on the road, and this having been approved by the 1831 officials, the change is now being prepared for by offering inducements for the best character of springs for this purpose. At this time, seventy miles of the Baltimore and Ohio have been completed, and it is the longest continuous line of railway in the world. The Washington branch, extending from the Relay House to the National Capitol, is assured, as the requisite charter has been obtained for it. A dividend, the first announced by a railroad company in America, is declared. The road is opened to Frederick the 1st of December, and of the total railway mileage constructed in the United States in 1831, of nearly ninety-nine miles, the Baltimore and Ohio built forty seven per cent., or forty-six and a half miles.

With the return of the Russian Commissioners, sent by the Czar to examine into the construction and management of the Baltimore and Ohio road, comes the imperial offer to Ross Winans to superintend the construction of the extensive system of railroads which has been decided upon in Russia. Winans has this under consideration, not as yet having decided to accept it. The Mine Hill and Schuylkill Haven road in Pennsylvania, with its fifteen miles of track, is completed at a cost of $181,000. It has white oak rails, carrying iron an inch and a half wide, and one-half an inch thick, the gauge being four feet eight and one-half inches. The sleepers rest upon stone rubble work in three parallel lines from one end of the road to the other. The Mount Carbon road in the same State is also finished, the construction being similar to the Schuylkill Haven line. In France the St. Etienne and Lyons railroad, connecting the two cities named, and thirty-four miles in length, is opened, the cost of the construction for the roadway alone reaching an average of $40,000 per mile. There is a double set of tracks, the rails being of wrought iron, fifteen feet long, three inches deep and two inches wide across the head, the upper and lower surfaces being parallel, similar to the Clarence rail, but the head at the bottom is formed only on one side. The rails weigh twenty-six and one half pounds to the yard, and are fixed to the chairs by means of compressed wooden wedges.

Dodd, of Glasgow, has built two locomotives for the Monkland and Kirkintilloch Railway in Scotland, which have demonstrated a capacity of drawing sixty tons at an average rate of four or five miles an hour, fully ten tons more than any other engine of like-sized cylin-

80

1831 ders with a pressure of fifty pounds has yet accomplished. The Stephensons, of Newcastle, have also produced two engines of great power, the "Samson" and "Goliath," both of which have been added to the motive power of the Liverpool and Manchester road. They are practically a four-wheel coupled development of the "Mercury," having cylinders of fourteen inches in diameter and a sixteen-inch stroke, the wheels being four feet six inches in diameter. The Glasgow and Garnkirk Railway in Scotland is opened, the first train being drawn by the locomotive "George Stephenson," and handled by Stephenson himself. The great success which has attended the Liverpool and Manchester road has stimulated railway enterprise throughout all Europe. Not only has it decided, in the most conclusive and practical manner, that railways are fitted for the conveyance of general merchandise, but with the development of the locomotive it has proven that they are capable of effecting a rapidity of transit greater than any other practical mode of traveling. The mails, which, despite every effort, could not be despatched to exceed ten miles an hour, are now carried with the greatest of ease at an average rate of fifteen miles an hour, and on, at the least, one extraordinary occasion, the Liverpool and Manchester doubled this speed over the entire line. With the exception of some of the railways in Scotland, all of the new systems are being constructed on the principle and of the same gauge as the Liverpool and Manchester.

To gratify the public interest in the locomotive in Philadelphia, the proprietor of Peale's Museum has had Mathias Baldwin make a model of one. This, simply from the published descriptions and sketches of those taking part in the Liverpool and Manchester trial, he has succeeded in doing to so successful an extent that the place is crowded to see the little engine running around the circular track made of pine boards and hoop iron, and laid upon the floor of the Museum. It has two small cars attached containing seats for four persons, and business is very brisk.

John Stephenson, the car builder of New York City, has designed and built for the New York and Harlem road, running from Prince street on the Bowery and thence to Yorkville and Harlem, a passenger car on the English railway plan, but lower, and hence easier of

"Hector"
1839

access. It has three compartments, each holding ten persons, and there is room on top for thirty more. It is drawn by a pair of horses, and produces a decided sensation, nothing like it having ever before been seen in the streets of a city in this country or abroad, and Stephenson says the result is so satisfactory that he will build several more of them.

As the year draws to a close the vexatious question as to what shall be done to render the English locomotives, which have been brought to America, of practical advantage on American roads, bids fair to be settled. Winans foreshadowed the ultimate recourse in the eight-wheel passenger car put on the Baltimore and Ohio during the midsummer. It is on two four-wheel trucks, and what more natural than his adopting this idea to the reconstruction of the "Herald" on the Baltimore and Susquehanna road? Removing the forward pair of wheels and replacing them with a four-wheel truck so arranged as to permit of swiveling exactly as his eight-wheel passenger car does when rounding the curves on the Baltimore and Ohio. This he follows out, and the "Herald" for the first time fills the bill. Meanwhile, John B. Jervis has reached exactly the same conclusions as regards the "Robert Fulton," the English locomotive on the Mohawk and Hudson road. It is difficult to say just which one of these two, or whether, as a matter of fact, Horatio Allen is not entitled to the distinction of having first thought out this plan. In either event, it is not new in principle in 1831, any more than in 1830 on the Quincy granite road, or in 1813 with the Chapmans in England. It had its origin in the first cars built to run on the road on which the first wheel was turned by a locomotive, the Merthyr Tydvil in South Wales, and these cars still exist to prove the fact that the "bogie" truck is primarily and historically an English, or rather a Welsh idea.

There is no question, however, as to the "Experiment," built at the West Point Foundry from the designs and plans of Jervis, being the first locomotive in the world constructed with a "bogie" or forward truck, and, as such a distinctive type of engine, different in many respects from all its predecessors. It is on six wheels instead of four, which has heretofore been the rule, although as a matter of fact not without some exceptions. Two are the driving wheels five feet in diameter, and the other four form the "bogie," or leading truck. The boiler is multi-

1831 tubular and horizontal, with the fire-box at the back end. There are two double-acting cylinders placed on the smoke-box far enough apart to permit the connecting rods to extend past the sides of the fire-box and connect to the cranks of the driving axle located in the rear. The valves are worked by two eccentrics mounted on a shifting sleeve surrounding the driving axle. One is for the forward and the other for the backward motion, and by the use of a lever conveniently located on the foot-plate either eccentric may be shifted to the right or left, and thrown into gear with one or the other of two collars or clutches fixed to the driving axle. The direction in which the engine moves depends on which collar is engaged by the eccentrics. Under the foot-plate there is a shaft connected by one set of arms to the eccentric rod and by the other to the valve rods, the latter extending forward over the foot-plate and past the side of the boiler to the steam chest. Handles are formed on the rods, and serve as a means for moving the valves by hand. The "Experiment" is running on the Mohawk and Hudson road, and already her performance is such as to indicate that she is anything but what her name implies. She is the fastest locomotive in the world, frequently making a mile a minute, and has reached the unprecedented rate for a short distance of eighty miles an hour. Almost simultaneously with the "Experiment's" appearance on the New York road, Allen places his "South Carolina" on the line after which it is named, and it is the first double-end loco-motive and the first eight-wheeled engine in the world. There are two pairs of drivers and two of truck wheels, one pair of the truck wheels being in front of the drivers and the other in the rear. Each group of two driving wheels and two truck wheels forms a separate pivoted truck, the idea being that such an arrangement is essential if the locomotive is to run in either direction with equal facility. The boiler has a fire-box at the center between the driving axles, and boiler shells of circular form; connected at each end of this fire-box extend, one forward, and the other back, two independent smoke-boxes, on each of which there is a smoke-stack. The cylinders are placed on the

83

Mercury 1842

First Locomotive Round-House, 1842. Mount Clare, Baltimore

James Murray

center line of the engine, one in each smoke-box, and each connecting-rod is 1831 coupled to a single crank on each driving-axle. Each valve is driven by two eccentrics, one for each direction. The eccentric-rods are notched and drive a rock-shaft which gives motion to the valve. The engineer can, by means of a single lever, reverse both engines simultaneously. One exhaust opens into each stack. The "South Carolina" was built at the West Point Foundry, and Allen, in explanation of his pronounced advance in construction, says that as more power is required in locomotives there must of necessity be more weight, and with this more wheels upon which to distribute it. Not only eight-wheel but ten-wheel locomotives, he declares, are requisite to meet the freight and passenger requirements of all long roads. Isaac Dripps, who has the direction of motive power on the Camden and Amboy, and who has not only the "John Bull" but several other English engines to contend with on that line, has adopted a plan to overcome their rigidity in rounding curves, and to improve their working generally. He introduces a pair of small pilot-wheels under a forward projection on the locomotive, and as an aid to this device one of the forward driving-wheels of the engine is so arranged as to revolve around the axle instead of turning with it.

Davis and Gardner have completed another locomotive, the "Atlantic," for the Baltimore and Ohio, and in it have embodied the results of a careful study of the performances of the "York" in connection with the improvements which have, from time to time, been added to the latter-named engine. The boiler has been radically changed, owing to the fact that the "York" is defective in the amount of heating surface and the circulation of the water. The supply of steam is consequently inadequate, and the deposit in the "cheese," as it is termed, cannot be removed. This trouble is obviated in the "Atlantic" by doing away with the "cheese" form altogether, and following closely the plan of the little Cooper boiler. Like the "York," the "Atlantic" is on four wheels; only two of them, however, are drivers. The boiler is vertical and multitubular. There are two double-acting cylinders set vertically and having connections from their upper ends to beams, or "grasshopper" legs, fulcrumed at their rear end to the boiler. Connecting-rods extend down from the front end of the beams to a shaft having a crank at each end and a gear at its cen-

84

Winans' "Mud Digger," 1844

ter.   This gear engages with another of half its diameter, keyed to the road-wheel axle.   The engine has valves, provided with outside lap, and the steam is worked through but two-thirds of the stroke at full pressure, the remainder of the stroke being completed by expansion.   The exhaust steam is discharged against the blades of a fan in such manner as to cause it to revolve rapidly, and produce a strong blast of air to aid the combustion of the anthracite coal used.   The engine weighs five and a half tons, and draws eighteen tons on five cars at an average speed of twelve miles an hour, but on several occasions has hauled thirty tons from Ellicott's Mills to Baltimore, a distance of thirteen miles, within an hour. With her tender only she has run at a speed of thirty miles or more per hour. Careful account is kept of the cost of operation, and it is found her daily labor involves an expense of but $16, while the same results accomplished with animal power costs $33.

First rail rolled in America
at Mt. Savage, Md.
1844

American Passenger Car
1844

The special committee appointed by the New York Legislature to examine into the plans of the various railroads in progress throughout the country reports that "the most approved method of constructing railways is the plan adopted by the Baltimore and Ohio Railroad Company."   Forty miles of the line are on granite sills, eight inches thick, fifteen wide, and of various lengths ; these are laid in trenches filled with broken stone.   Other portions of the road are upon stone blocks and still others on a wooden base.   The string-pieces throughout are six inches square, the iron bars or rails are fifteen feet long, two and a quarter inches wide, five-eighths of an inch thick, and cut off obliquely at the ends.   The first thirteen miles of the road are by far the most difficult and expensive to build, the grading and masonry alone costing an average of $46,354 per mile.   The average cost for the entire line thus far, counting everything, is about $30,000 per mile. In the construction of the main line from Baltimore to Point of Rocks, seventy-three miles, to which it is now completed, every mode hitherto suggested by science or experience has been tested, and thus the work may be truly said to solve most of the problems which have presented themselves to this time.   The iron on the granite sill, the wood and iron on stone blocks, the wood and iron on wooden sleepers supported by broken stone, the same supported by longitudinal ground sills, the log sill formed of the trunks of trees worked to a surface on one side to receive the iron, and supported by wooden sleepers crosswise,

85

Gooch's
Great Western
1846

together with wrought-iron rails, have all been laid in different portions of the line in actual operation, and are therefore subjected to the most practical of tests. It is well said that the Baltimore and Ohio is the railroad primary school of America. Steel springs are another innovation first introduced in locomotive construction on this road by being placed as an experiment on the engine " York." Their utility was at once demonstrated by greatly diminishing the jar and consequent injury to the road. No accidents have as yet occurred on the line, although upwards of one hundred and forty thousand people have travelled on it, and at this time, early in 1832, it is the longest railway in existence. Now, however, a most 1832 unfortunate event transpires! The Court of Appeals decides that the injunction obtained by the Chesapeake and Ohio Canal Company against the railroad company shall stand until the Canal Company locates its route from Point of Rocks to Harper's Ferry, on the ground of " prior and paramount" rights on the part of the canal company. This brings the westward advance of the Baltimore and Ohio to a complete standstill.

The Camden and Amboy road is finished from Bordentown to Amboy, a distance of twenty-six and a half miles. As on the Baltimore and Ohio, a variety of plans of construction have been followed. Edge-rails of wrought iron, weighing thirty-six pounds to the yard, and of unusual strength have been laid on some portions of the road. They rest upon stone blocks two feet square. Other rails are of English rolled iron, sixteen feet long, two and one-eighth inches wide at the bottom, and three and one-half inches deep, and with a web half an inch thick. These rails weigh forty pounds to the yard, and are attached to the stone blocks and sleepers by means of nails or pins driven into wooden plugs at the sides. Chairs are dispensed with, the rails being secured by clamps of iron at the extremity of each bar. The Stevens T-rail is also being put down. The whole distance from Camden to Amboy, by the line as run, is sixty-one miles, and it is almost mathematically straight. The Newcastle and Frenchtown road, connecting the Delaware with the Chesapeake, is also opened in 1832. The rail used is of English make, and about the same as that laid on the Camden and Amboy. In nine miles of the line the rails rest upon granite blocks, twenty inches in length and twelve inches square, each block weighing three hundred and sixty pounds. On the Allegheny Portage Railroad, a system of signalling is in use which is somewhat unique. A large post, called

86

Winans' "Delaware"
1846

a center-post, is set up half-way between two turnouts, and the rule is that when two drivers meet with their cars on the single track, the one that has gone beyond the center-post has the right to proceed, and the other must go back to the turnout. As the line is very crooked, and the driver cannot see far ahead, the practice is to go very slowly, until he gets in sight of the center-post, fearing he may have to turn back, but when the post is sighted he whips up and makes all possible speed to get beyond it before the other fellow coming in the opposite direction can do so. The result is that two cars, more or less frequently come together with terrific force, and in these wild dashes for right of way, one man has been killed and others injured. The line of the Portage Railroad extends from Johnstown, on the Conemaugh River, a distance of nearly thirty-seven miles, to Holliday's on the Juniata. There are ten inclined planes on the route. The rails used weigh thirty-nine and a half pounds to the yard, and for about one-half the length of the road are laid on stone blocks, the other half resting on wooden stringers.

Richard Norris

There are sixty-seven roads, varying in length from a hundred yards to twenty-two and a half miles, in actual operation in Pennsylvania, but not one is constructed with iron rails exclusively. The great majority are entirely of wood, with not a particle of iron in their composition. The English rails imported for the Philadelphia and Columbia road, cost, delivered in Philadelphia, fifty dollars a ton, and weigh forty-one and a quarter pounds to the yard. The cast-iron chairs weigh fifteen pounds each, the nails or bolts ten ounces, and the two wrought-iron wedges to each chair also ten ounces. Seventeen miles of track are laid on stone sills, and the remainder, including that portion in the city of Philadelphia, on wooden sleepers, placed crosswise in trenches filled with broken stone. The first car put on the West Chester branch of the road is a four-wheel conveyance, built at Wilmington, Delaware, and having five seats inside, running across the whole width of the car. The drivers' seats at each end are of equal length, and have but little elevation above those inside. Each seat provides ample space for five persons, and in all there is room for thirty-four passengers. Along either side of the exterior of the car there is a platform nine inches wide, which affords standing-room for twenty persons.

87

Norris "Chesapeake" 1846

When the question of the arrangement of the seats in the eight-wheel cars on the Baltimore and Ohio is before the directors, the proposition to make an entrance at each end, with an aisle down the centre, and provide seats for two persons on each side, is received with much opposition, on the ground that the passengers would be able to expectorate at will upon the extent of floor provided by the aisle, and would make it one long spittoon. This view of the results of a decision favorable to the aisle, settles the discussion, and the car is finished with doors on the side and in divisions about half the height to the roof, the seats extending the full width of the car, provision being made for the conductor to reach the passengers from a narrow ledge running lengthwise on the outside.

The Saratoga and Schenectady road, an extension of the Mohawk and Hudson, twenty-two miles in length, and intended chiefly for passengers, is finished. The track consists of a strap rail on wooden stringers resting on stone blocks, for a distance of three miles, and on wooden sleepers for the remainder. The Legislature of the State of New York has granted a petition for the incorporation of the New York and Erie, but connection with any railroad in the State of New Jersey is especially forbidden. The cost of that part of the Philadelphia, Germantown, and Norristown road, between Philadelphia and Germantown, six miles in length, is placed at $300,000 per mile. The rails are of English make, fifteen feet long, and weigh thirty-nine pounds to the yard. This rail rests in cast-iron chairs secured to stone blocks by iron bolts terminating in screws or nuts. Melted lead is used in lieu of wooden plugs for securing the bolts in the stones. Sleepers are not used on any part of the line, the stone blocks, containing two cubic feet each, being placed in pits containing broken stone three feet apart from center to center.

Work is begun on the Boston and Lowell road in Massachusetts, and seventy-five miles of the South Carolina road have been completed and placed in operation. The Lexington and Ohio Railroad Company has seven miles of road under contract on a line from Lexington to Louisville; and eight miles of the Paterson and Hudson, in New Jersey, are graded. Already one hundred and sixteen charters for railroads projected, to exceed five miles in length, have been granted in the United States.

An order from the Philadelphia, Germantown, and Norristown road for a locomotive has stimulated Mathias Baldwin to the study of the English engines in Philadelphia, and

Trevithick's "Cornwall" 1847

to an extensive series of experiments. The result is that in 1832, the first Baldwin locomotive and the first successful American-built locomotive in Pennsylvania makes its appearance. Baldwin calls his engine the "Old Ironsides," and the general model indicates that her designer has made a close investigation of the "John Bull," the English engine on the Camden and Amboy. In other words, the "Old Ironsides" is of the Stephenson "Planet" type, and can scarcely be regarded as an American locomotive, except in the fact that it is of American construction. In efficiency, however, it is a long way ahead of any English construction seen in America, and the "Old Ironsides" can give the "Bull," the "Fulton," the "Herald," or any other Stephenson locomotive now in America, odds and win easily. The English makers build fine locomotives for their home roads, the construction of many of them being particularly good and strong, and as a consequence the results obtained are such as to greatly advance the railway progress of Europe, but for some reason not a single English engine has been a success on the American continent in anything like the form received from the builders. This may be owing to the fact that the situation in America has not been comprehended, or that the demand from the United States is characteristically impetuous, and thus sufficient time is not given to fully complete the work. So while the "Old Ironsides" is of the Stephenson type, it is not much more English than this statement implies, that is to say—in model. She is upon four wheels, one pair of which are drivers and placed forward of the fire-box. There are two horizontal cylinders fixed on the outside of the smoke-box and connected with cranks on the driving-axle. The frame is outside of the wheels, the axle-boxes being carried by pedestals. Each of the inside guides is hollow and serves as a pump. The valves are each worked by one eccentric, through a rock-shaft under the foot-board. A lever is provided for reversing the engine by lifting the eccentric rods from the lower to the upper arms of the rock shaft. The boiler is multitubular. The "Old Ironsides" has developed a speed of thirty miles an hour, and is the popular feature of the Germantown line.

James, of New York, has finished his sixth locomotive, although four were for turnpikes, not rail roads. This engine of 1832, in an incident, or rather an accident, of construction, and in the principle it, for the first time indicates, bids fair to awaken a good deal of interest. Samuel B. Dougherty is James's foreman now, and the two stop at no hours or days in pushing

Jenny Lind 1848

the work on the locomotive to get it ready for service on the Baltimore and Ohio road. The "James" is on four wheels, the boiler is vertical and conical in form, without tubes, and has a fire-box surrounded by a water space. Two double-acting cylinders of ten inches diameter and ten-inch stroke are placed at an angle of thirty degrees from the horizontal on a wooden frame forward of the boiler. The piston-rods extend through the back or lower end of the cylinders and are connected to cross-heads running on flat guides. The connecting-rods are coupled to cranks on a shaft almost directly over the forward axle. Two gear-wheels of different diameter are mounted near the center of this axle and driven by a spline or feather, so they may be moved by hand, to engage either one of a large and small gear keyed to the axle of the road-wheels. The combination is such that a large gear may be thrown into gear with a small one, or a small one with a large one, as deemed best for the work to be done. The steam-chests are on top of the cylinders, and each contains a slide valve having three-quarters of an inch outside lap and driven through a link by two eccentrics on the shaft. The position of the link is controlled by the engineer through a reverse lever, and a weight is fixed at the end of the lever to hold the link up or down, according to the direction the locomotive is to move. No provision is made for varying the point of cut-off, although it is known that the link may be adjusted for this purpose. The link was devised by James as a means for reversing, but it was found while setting the valves that the mechanism would give a variable cut-off. James told Dougherty to set the valves with one and one-sixteenth inch lead, but not to put the steam-chest covers on until he—James—had inspected the valves. When James examined the valves he discovered a one and a quarter-inch lead, and had Dougherty turn the engine over to the other end. This was done and the lead was found to be one and a quarter-inch at that end also, and an examination ensued to learn the cause of the greater lead, as Dougherty declared he had followed the instructions given him to set the valves with one and a sixteenth lead. On inspection it was found that the link was not all the way down, and this led to the discovery that it would vary the cut-off, James recognizing this fact with the remark, "Yes, it will cut off, but I guess it don't amount to much; however, we will put the lap on the valves." The exhaust of the engine is into the smoke-arch at the base of the stack. The frame carries the fuel-boxes and tank, and the locomotive has two pumps for feeding the boiler, and requires no tender.

Colonel Long, nothing daunted or discouraged by the unsuccessful results of his first engine, renews his efforts, and the firm of Long and Norris, the successors of the American Steam Carriage Company, bring out a locomotive named the "Black Hawk," and it is placed upon the Philadelphia and Germantown road. It burns hard coal, with natural draught only; this, however, is increased by the introduction of a very high chimney so arranged as to be lowered from an altitude of twenty or more feet from the rails to the height requisite for passing under the bridges which cross the railroad. The boiler is also an innovation. It has a fire-box formed with water-sides, and made so that it may be detached from the waist or cylindrical portion. There are two cylinders, twenty inches in diameter, placed close together and forming the roof of the fire-box. A notch is cut half way between these two cylinders on their lower half diameters, about midway of the length of the fire-box directly over the fire, and from these notches flues of about two inches diameter pass through the water-space of the cylindrical portion of the boiler to the smoke-box. These flues are about seven feet long. Besides passing through the flues the fire passes also under the lower halves of the cylinder portion of the boiler, a double sheet-iron casing filled between with clay forming the lower portion of the flue and connecting it with the smoke-box. The "Black Hawk" is on four wheels, the drivers, four and a half feet in diameter, being in front of the fire-box. Inside cylinders, a double-crank axle, springs on the front axle and the cam cut-off are other features of the engine, which is a successful one as regards its performances.

In England Bury has placed the "Liver," with cylinders eleven by sixteen inches and drivers five feet in diameter, on the Liverpool and Manchester Railway. Galloway and Borman, of Glasgow, have built for the same line the "Caledonian," with four five-foot wheels, coupled, and without the crank-axle, and they have placed the cylinders vertically in front of the smoke-box. Twelve-ton engines have been introduced on the Stockton and Darlington road, and when worked at moderate speed have been demonstrated to be sufficiently powerful for hauling the heaviest coal-trains. The railway from Roane to Andrezieux, in France, forty-two miles, is finished. Hawthorne's first locomotive, the "Coronation," on the Stockton and Darlington, is ballasted with iron weights in the rear to steady it, as all the gearing, including the cylinders, is in front and projecting ahead

The "Dragon"
1848

"Pioneer"
The First Locomotive in Chicago, 1848

of the leading wheels. The "Wilberforce," designed by Hackworth, and built by the Hawthornes, has also been put into service on the Stockton and Darlington. It has a boiler thirteen feet long and forty-four inches in diameter. The fire-box is in a tube twenty-nine inches in diameter and nine feet long, the fire-door being at the same end as the chimney. At the end of the tube farthest from the chimney the flame is divided and the heat returns through a group of copper tubes on each side of the fire-box. A smoke-box receives the combustion from both groups of tubes and communicates with the chimney in the usual way. The cylinders are fourteen and a half inches in diameter and the stroke sixteen inches. The piston-rods work through the lower cylinder-heads and are connected by short connecting rods to cranks fixed at right angles to each other upon the ends of a stout shaft revolving in bearings upon the frame. From this shaft motion is imparted by coupling rods to three pairs of wheels, each four feet in diameter, and mounted on springs. The steam pressure is from thirty-six to sixty pounds to the square inch, and the weight eleven and three-quarter tons. This engine is used exclusively for freight, but the "Arrow," also designed by Hackworth, is of another type, and frequently draws the express at a sixty-mile an hour rate. This engine is quite an exceptional one, having cylinders twenty-one inches in diameter with a stroke of only seven inches.

Hardly any two of Hackworth's engines have been alike. Stephenson, on the other hand, when getting hold of a good idea, repeats it over and over again. The result is Stephenson is making lots of money and Hackworth is not; but the latter is compelling locomotive designers all over the world to step right lively to keep up with him.

Stephenson has put his first locomotive, the "Comet," on the Leicester and Swannington road, it having been shipped by sea from Newcastle to Hull and thence by canal to Leicester. The cylinders of this engine are twelve by sixteen inches, the coupled wheels five feet in diameter, the wheel-base five feet three inches, and the length of the engine over all sixteen feet. The chimney of the "Comet" was thirteen feet high when it reached the road, but was knocked off in a tunnel on the opening day and then reduced about six inches. Stephenson has designed a passenger

Crampton's "Liverpool"
1848

92

car for the Columbia road in Pennsylvania, the drawings being now in hand. It has no roof, but is divided into compartments with seats running crosswise, and the sides of the car are high enough to keep passengers from falling out. The baggage goes under the seats, small doors being provided for getting in and out. Portable steps are designed to enable the patrons of the road to obey the command, "All aboard." Several of these cars have been built by the Stephensons for the Stockton and Darlington road.

A wood car has been added to the equipment of the Baltimore and Ohio road, and it is the first eight-wheel freight car in the world. It is on two four-wheel trucks, the same as the passenger-car "Columbus," but as it is drawn by the locomotive "Atlantic," an arrangement has been perfected by which it may be coupled to the engine as well as to other cars. Winans built it, and has the designs in readiness for two new eight-wheel passenger-cars. The experiments made in providing conveyances for passengers on the Baltimore and Ohio are numerous, and several of the results very striking.

1833   In 1833 the "Traveler," Davis & Gardner's third engine for the Baltimore and Ohio, is constructed especially for freight purposes, and as such is the first of the type in service. It has four wheels of equal diameter, all coupled, two double-acting cylinders placed vertically, with piston-rods extending through the upper heads, and two links connected to "grasshopper" legs or walking-beams, the rear ends of which are pivoted on the boiler. The front end of each leg, just forward of the cylinder connection, is coupled to a connecting-rod, which extends down to an intermediate shaft, having a crank at each end, and a spur-gear at its center. In front of this shaft there is another, of sufficient length to reach outside of the frame, having cranks on each end to which coupling-rods are attached and extend back to cranks on the outside of the wheel axle. A frame is interposed between the wheels and the cranks, to which pedestals are bolted for carrying axle-boxes. The forward shaft has a gear at its center, which runs into the spur-gear on the intermediate shaft. The boiler is of the vertical, multitubular type, and is carried in the center of a frame between the wheels. There is a fan blower over the fire-door, and in the center of the case surrounding it a space filled with tubes around which the feed-water circulates on its way to the boiler. One end of the blower contains a fan wheel, against the

93

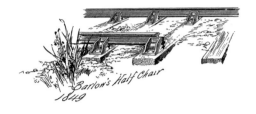

Barlow's Half Chair
1849

blades of which the exhaust steam is projected, causing it to revolve and also to revolve a similar fan secured to the same shaft, and in the other end of the case. This latter fan has openings in its case, through which air is drawn and forced through a pipe to the fire. The steam passes from the fan wheel through the tubes in the feed-water chamber, where it gives off heat to the surrounding water and then escapes by a pipe to the atmosphere. The valves are each operated by two cams on the intermediate shaft. Each pair of cams has one yoke which may be thrown by foot-pressure to become engaged with the cam set for the forward or backward motion of the engine as desired. The foot-pressure moves the cam laterally, and a lever is used for adjusting the yoke so the cam can enter it, being a feeler. The "Traveler" has equaled expectations from the day she was first steamed up. The differences between the Baltimore and Ohio Company and the Chesapeake and Ohio Canal Company have been adjusted, and construction westward from Point of Rocks is resumed. The final act of the Legislature to enable the railroad company to construct its line to Washington is secured, and the contracts awarded for the building of the viaduct over the Patapsco at Relay.

Trouble being occasioned the company by delay in receiving locomotives ordered, through the lack of facilities at York, where Davis and Gardner have several under contract, the directors decide to build their own locomotive shops at Mount Clare, where new engines can be constructed and old ones repaired when necessary. This plan is put into execution, and Davis is induced to favorably consider an arrangement to remove to Baltimore and carry out his contract work there under satisfactory terms as to the use of shops, machinery, etc., belonging to the railroad company.

In England the financial affairs of the Liverpool and Manchester are creating some criticism, the total expenditures on the line to the end of 1832 being £1,200,000, or six millions of dollars, while the three years' actual business done is in the aggregate only about one-third of what was calculated would be the total of a single year, and the cost of transport has been eight times greater than Messrs. Stephenson and Locke estimated it would be. However, these statements do not affect the progress of the road in getting the best that is to be had, and, despite depression in stocks and that sort of thing, the advance in ex-

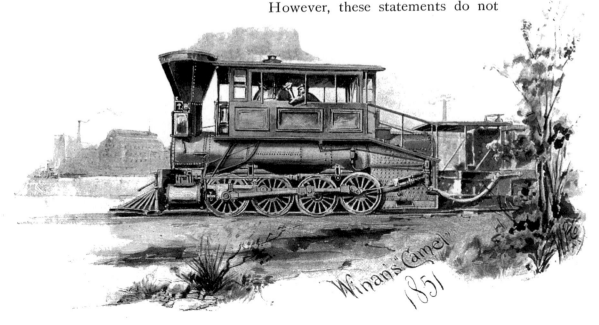

Winan's Camel
1851

cellence continues. Until recently the locomotives on the road were usually constructed with a double crank for the two main wheels, which were flanged. But this having been found objectionable, owing to the crank-axles becoming strained or broken by the friction of the flanges against the rails at various points of the line, Robert Stephenson does away with the flanges on the driving wheels in several instances, and places another pair of smaller wheels with flanges behind the drivers. These new wheels are under the fire-box end of the boiler, and it is believed will add greatly to the efficiency of the engine. With plain tires on the drivers it becomes practicable to work an engine with a wheel-base of ten or twelve feet around the sharpest curves on the road. Private carriages are taken on the road and transported with their passengers from place to place, by means of flat frames mounted upon car-wheels, and constructed to receive almost any kind of a vehicle and carry it safely. The regular coaches in use have compartments for three classes of passengers. Those for first class seating eighteen and the others twenty-four each. The latter, however, have no covering or roof.

West Jersey R. R.
1850

Experience on the Liverpool and Manchester having proved that the six-wheel freight locomotive is superior to the four-wheeled, the Stephensons have constructed for the road a new type of passenger-engine on this principle. It is practically upon the model of the "Mercury," but with the addition of the smaller pair of trailing wheels under the foot-plate. This engine is named the "Patentee," from the fact that it is the first constructed by Stephenson under his patent for six-wheeled engines without flanges upon the middle pair of wheels. The cylinders of the "Patentee" are twelve by eighteen inches, and the driving wheels five feet in diameter. Stephenson has also introduced in this locomotive his first steam brake. The admission of the steam into a brake cylinder raises a piston, which, through a lever and rod, elevates a toggle just between the brake blocks, forcing them against the tread of the wheels.

Jervis concluding, for various reasons, to have a locomotive built in England, enters into an arrangement with the Stephensons to construct it from plans sent over by him, and thus the first engine with the "bogie," or forward truck, seen in Europe is through the instrumentality of an American. It is the "Davy Crockett," for the Saratoga and Schenectady. In general make up it is much after the style of Jervis's first engine, the "Experiment," having the

95

Eddy's "Gilmore" 1851

four wheels in a pivoted truck forward and a single pair of driving wheels behind the fire-box.

Robert Stephenson deprecates the procedure in the United States as regards the continued tendency to light-weight motive power, and his letter received by Robert L. Stevens implies, if it does not so state, that the reason for the diminishing orders for English engines is from the realization that they have been found too heavy for the wooden stringer and strap-iron lines in America, and this situation cannot be changed, he says, until there is a very decided betterment of American permanent way as a whole. He writes: "I am sorry the feeling in the United States in favor of light railways is so general. In England we are making each succeeding railway stronger and more substantial. Small engines are losing ground and large ones are daily demonstrating that powerful engines are the most economical." He sends a sketch of one of his latest locomotives weighing nine tons, and capable, he claims, of taking a hundred tons gross load at a speed of from sixteen to seventeen miles an hour.

Up to the present year the locomotive fireman in Europe, in addition to his ordinary stoking duties, has had to pull a bell or blow a trumpet when signaling approach, but William Stevens, of the Dowlais Iron Works in South Wales, has introduced the first steam whistle, and it is immediately recognized as a long-felt want.

Roberts's "Experiment," constructed for the Liverpool and Manchester road, has cylinders placed vertically over the leading wheels, the motion of the cross-heads being communicated to the crank-pins upon the driving wheels by means of connecting-rods and bell-cranks. The leading wheels have outside and the driving wheels inside bearings. The cylinders are eleven by sixteen inches and the drivers five feet in diameter. The "Experiment" has no eccentrics to actuate the valves, a short lever on the bell-crank giving the required motion through a long rod to a rocking gear on the foot-plate. The "Earl of Airlee," built by Carmichael, of Dundee, Scotland, is upon the Dundee and Newtyle Railroad, and is the first of the English-made locomotives with the "bogie" truck, or at the least on that principle. In this instance the driving wheels, a single pair four feet six inches in diameter, are forward, and the four wheels constituting the truck in the rear. The cylinders are vertical, eleven inches

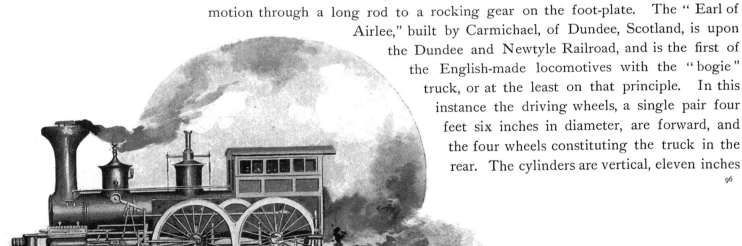

Milholland's "Illinois" 1852

in diameter, with a stroke of eighteen inches. The "Hercules," the Stephenson six-wheel engine delivered to the Leicester and Swannington road, with cylinders fourteen by eighteen inches, has had the flanges removed from the driving wheels, and the working steam pressure increased from fifty-five to sixty pounds. The "Dundee," constructed by Roberts for the Dundee and New-tyle, in its short stroke is a pronounced departure from the long-entertained idea of English builders of the value of the long stroke, and correspondingly long connecting-rods. Stephenson has introduced a small pair of trailing wheels behind the fire-box of the "Mercury," and it is now a six-wheel engine, the Stephensons having become so thoroughly convinced of the advantages of the six-wheel locomotives over the four-wheel, that they not only build all their new engines of this type but so alter all the old ones of their make they can control. The English engines are, as a rule, now constructed to carry a steam pressure of sixty pounds to the square inch. In America, the standard is one hundred and twenty to one hundred and thirty pounds. Dixon, of the Stockton and Darlington road, has introduced for the first time hard brass in the place of copper for tubes, and this has effected an incalculable saving in the repairs of coke-burning engines.

The South Carolina Railroad has one hundred and thirty-seven miles of road in operation. It completed the first one hundred miles of railway in existence, and is now by several miles the longest in the world. Experience on the Baltimore and Ohio, notwithstanding the movement of the trains is much more smooth and steady on the part laid with granite sills than where the iron is upon wooden stringers, has demonstrated that the stone sills are much more expensive to hold the rails to than the wood, and it has been about decided to replace the stone with wood. The road is open for business to Harper's Ferry. Long and Norris are enlarging their shops in Philadelphia, and Colonel Long has patented the use of

a supplementary expansion valve which, by an additional lap on the valve, will cut off at either one-half or five-eighths of the stroke. He likewise has a patent for an arrangement whereby when two horizontal inside cylinders are employed one slide valve will do for both; still an-

other on the telescopic or "slip" chimney for locomotives, and in apparent ignorance of what James has done the Colonel claims the first use of four fixed cams, each having nearly the action of the common eccentric. All these features Long introduced in the "Black Hawk," and his patents are to protect them. McIlvaine has perfected an arrangement for keeping sparks from the flues of locomotives in which wood is used as fuel; and Mitchell, of Philadelphia, has taken out a patent on what he terms the Pennsylvania edge rail and chair.

When the Liverpool and Manchester Railroad was first constructed there were twenty-two regular and seven occasional stage coaches between the two cities, with combined capacity for six hundred and eighty-eight passengers. The railway has averaged eleven hundred passengers per day since it was opened. The fare by coach was ten shillings inside and five shillings outside. The fare by railway is five shillings inside and three and six outside. Time by coach four hours; by rail, an hour and three quarters.

The progress in the direction of steam carriages for common roads in England still continues, and there are at the close of 1833 no less than nineteen under way in London. The success met with in these vehicles, particularly in the way of speed, is a constant incentive to the locomotive builders to improve their engines in this respect. The construction as well of these carriages affords object lessons of no ordinary importance. One of them, the "Macerone," has run upward of seventeen hundred miles without repairs.

The "Thomas Jefferson," the third of the Davis engines, and largely the 1834 duplicate of the "Traveler," has been placed in service on the Baltimore and Ohio road. Baldwin, who for some months has been at work on his second locomotive, the "E. L. Miller," for the South Carolina road, delivers it in February, 1834. It is in no wise like the first Baldwin engine, the "Old Ironsides," the maker having abandoned all tendency toward English types, and the "Miller" is a thoroughly American locomotive. It is upon six wheels, one pair, the drivers, four and a half feet in diameter, and the four front wheels combined in a swiveling truck. Baldwin introduces in this engine his invention of the half crank, the axle with it being placed back of the fire-box. The drivers are of brass cast from solid bell metal. The cylinders are ten inches in diameter, with a sixteen-inch stroke, and the boiler has

a high dome over the fire-box, also an innovation. Not long after the "Miller" Baldwin has his third engine ready, the "Lancaster," built to the order of the Columbia road in Pennsylvania. It is practically the same as the "Miller" except as to the driving wheels, the experiment with brass not being repeated. The "Lancaster" weighs seven and a half tons and is demonstrating greater power than any other locomotive yet built in the United States. One track of the Columbia and Philadelphia road is finished throughout its entire length. At the formal opening the two trains consist of thirty four-wheel cars each, seating sixteen persons each, eight on a side. These cars are mostly of stage-coach pattern, having been built by makers of such vehicles. Baldwin has taken out a patent for ground steam-tight joints for the steam-pipes of locomotives, doing away with the old practice of making them tight by red lead packing. Miller also has a patent of importance, on an arrangement for so connecting the engine and tender that a portion of the weight of the latter shall be carried by the former, and in this manner add to the weight on the driving wheels. The plan increases the adhesion of the engine in proportion to its load, and makes possible a proportion of traction to the weight, hitherto unknown.

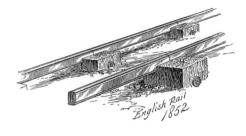

English Rail 1852

In England the year is everywhere emphasizing that engines on but four wheels are objectionable by reason of the considerable weight of the driving wheels upon the rails, and because of their unsteadiness with a short wheel-base, as well as on account of the increased danger to the engine and train in case of the breaking of an axle. The lead of the Stephensons in adopting six wheels is in reality no more than a return to Hackworth's practice of seven years ago. For the past four years the advancement of the English engine has not been such as to do away with very many defects which are now being more sensibly felt than ever, owing to the demand for faster time, for more power, and a higher standard of efficiency generally. The eccentrics as a rule are loose on the crank axle, and are held to their work only by stops, or "drivers," as they are termed, and there is a great shock in reversing, especially at high speed. It is common, too, to attach the draw iron directly to the fire-box, and thus subject the boiler to all the shocks due to the inequalities in the draught of the train. The grate bars are widely spaced and do not fit accurately to the

99

Bristol & Exeter Express 1852

sides of the fire-box, and as a consequence, much fuel is lost, particularly as there is neither ash-pan nor damper. In many instances the cylinders are still fastened mainly to the smoke-box, and the boiler is attached to the frame in a manner which produces heavy strains upon it when the engine is fired up. The chimneys are yet very large, generally thirteen and a half inches in diameter for engines with eleven-inch cylinders. On the other hand the blast pipes are, as a rule, small, being two and a quarter inches in diameter and carried some distance up the chimney. In nearly all cases steam is admitted during almost the entire length of the stroke of the pistons, and as the exhaust does not open until the end of the stroke, there is considerable loss from back pressure as well as from not working expansively. It is not uncommon to run with the fire door open, and the engines are often reversed with a full head of steam on the pistons. The low pressure of fifty pounds per square inch, adopted from considerations of safety, is a disadvantage, and it is becoming generally recognized that other precautions will have to be taken to enable the adoption of the American practice of carrying at the least double this pressure. The wheels, generally speaking, have a small wearing surface in proportion to the resistance they have to withstand, and the tires are coned to an extent which causes constant and trying strains upon the entire locomotive. The recourse to the six-wheel type is a recognition at last of the actual movements of a locomotive with a wheel base of only about five feet, and with widely spread cylinders and more or less unbalanced weights.

The first of Forrester's engines from the Vauxhall Foundry at Liverpool is the "Swiftsure," and in it is the primary introduction in England of the combination of outside cylinders and six wheels, with the connecting-rods working upon outside cranks. The "Swiftsure" has four eccentrics, after the plan of Forrester's patent, each of the four having a forked or "gab-end," and a vertical position. The cylinders are eleven inches in diameter with an eighteen-inch stroke, the driving wheels five feet in diameter, and the total length of frame seventeen feet. In consequence of the extreme distance from center to center of the cylinders (seven feet and one inch) and the unbalanced driving wheels, this engine oscillates in a very serious and dangerous manner, even when driven at

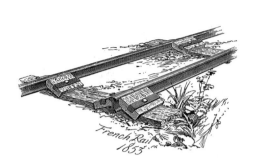

French Rail
1853

Norris-Phleger
1853

moderate speed. The Forresters have this year, in addition to this, built three four-wheel engines, the "Dublin," "Kingstown" and "Vauxhall," known on the Dublin and Kingstown road as the "Boxers," and like the "Swiftsure," they are very unsteady.

Stephenson's new engine the "Atlas," with six wheels all coupled, has been delivered to the Leicester and Swannington road. She has cylinders sixteen by twenty inches, and without the tender weighs in working order seventeen tons, being the largest and heaviest locomotive to this time. The "Atlas" is also the first freight or "goods" engine with six coupled wheels and inside cylinders. The boiler has a straight top, is jacketed with polished oak strips bound on with brass hoops, and the engine has a steam trumpet. The wheels are four feet six inches in diameter, the center pair without flanges. Bury has built the "Liverpool," for the same line. It has four wheels, four feet six inches in diameter, and cylinders twelve by eighteen inches. A peculiar feature is two eccentrics on the leading axle, with eccentric rods extending through the smoke-box, in passages provided for the purpose, to the valve levers located behind the buffer beam. The reversing gear is operated by four handles, two to work the valves by hand, one "gab-handle" to throw the small ends of the eccentric rods into or out of gear, and one to move the two eccentrics. Roberts's "Hibernia," for the Dublin and Kingstown road, is one of three delivered at the same time, the others being the "Manchester" and "Britannia." All are, like the "Experiment," made by Roberts for the opening of this line, and distinguished for a new and bold departure in a novel location of the cylinders, and for the short stroke and parallel motion. These locomotives are further noteworthy from the fact that their frames are stronger, fastenings better, bearing surfaces larger and of superior design, while machine work is substituted to a great extent in place of the hand fitting more commonly employed by the north country engineer.

The annual cost so far of repairing the Liverpool and Manchester locomotives is equal to about two per cent. upon the total capital stock of the Company which is something over seven millions of dollars. There are now thirty engines on the line and of these ten are useless. The sum paid for repairs last year would have purchased twenty new engines at the prevailing price,

101

£778. The repairs the first half of this year have cost equal to twelve new engines. The expense of the fuel this year is not one-third of that for locomotive repairs, while the repairs of track and road-bed, costly as they necessarily are, are not as large as the repairs on engines. Heavier rails are being substituted for those originally laid. The nine- and ten-ton engines, even after adding the extra pair of wheels, are found still too severe upon the track, and the new iron is sixty-six pounds to the yard.

The Locks and Canals Company at Lowell, Massachusetts, has finished the "Patrick" for the Boston and Lowell road. It is strongly suggestive of the English "Planet" type, having cylinders eleven by sixteen inches, five-foot driving wheels with three-foot leading wheels, a boiler two feet ten inches in diameter, and weighs eleven tons. The "Patrick," as well as the "Concord," "Nashua," "Medford" and "Suffolk," which follow on the Boston and Lowell, are all wood burners. On the South Carolina road Allen has an open platform car, which he places in front of the locomotive when running at night, and on this car, surrounded by sand, he burns pine knots to light the road ahead. The first freight cars on the Boston and Albany road are just large enough to hold two hogsheads of molasses. A director named Hammond, who wants to order eighty-five of these cars and insists that they will be needed, is regarded with much suspicion as to his sanity by his fellows. In France an atmospheric locomotive is attracting attention, and experiments with it lead some people to argue that the steam locomotive is to be superseded.

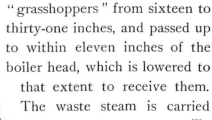

The great granite viaduct on the Baltimore and Ohio over the Patapsco at Relay, consisting of eight elliptical arches each of fifty-eight feet span, and the roadway sixty-six feet from the water-level, is completed and is the largest structure of the kind in the United States. In the estimates of the cost of the work its designer and engineer, Benjamin H. Latrobe, came within the actual expenses of construction. The "Arabian," Davis's fourth engine for the Baltimore and Ohio, is in service, having been built in the company's shops at Mount Clare. In the "Arabian" the tubes have been lengthened over those hitherto used in the "grasshoppers" from sixteen to thirty-one inches, and passed up to within eleven inches of the boiler head, which is lowered to that extent to receive them. The waste steam is carried

Great Northern R'y of France
1853

McQueen's 8 Wheeler
1853

to the fan chamber by a hollow belt winding round the boiler, and the feed pipe is contained within it, so that the water is heated before it is pumped into the boiler. The "Arabian's" cylinders are twelve by twenty-two inches, and her weight seven and a half tons. The gearing is similar to that of the "Atlantic" but with a separate axle on the frame to carry the pinion and spur wheel, as in the "Traveler." Other locomotives, the "Mercury," the "Antelope" and the "American," are placed on the road, in 1834, the last two named being produced by Charles Reeder, of Baltimore, from the drawings and designs of Davis and Winans. Strenuous efforts have been made by foreign builders, through their special representatives sent to the United States for the purpose, to induce the Baltimore and Ohio Company to permit English locomotives on the road, but the board has invariably decided otherwise. In conformity with this rule and the principle established when steam-power was determined upon, an order has just been given for eight additional locomotives, all of them of American make throughout.

Winans, who, since his first eight-wheel car, the "Columbus," in 1831, has been working upon the details of the trucks so as to make them available for use in cars of much greater length, has patented the plan put into execution in the car "Dromedary." By connecting the axle-boxes of the two pairs of wheels together with two strong springs, one on each side, and connected by a transverse bolster carrying the swivel pivots socket no other frame is employed. The pioneer railway in Bavaria, and which extends from Nuremberg to Fürth, is formally opened with timely observances.

The Baltimore and Ohio is completed to Washington — opened for business August 25th, and the National Capital has its first rail connection with the outer world. Simultaneously with this event Winans adds another eight-wheel passenger-car, with trucks still further improved through the lowering of the body of the car and thus insuring augmented steadiness. This car, the "Comet," will seat forty passengers, and has an aisle through the center with cushioned seats for two persons on either side. The backs of the seats are attached by long iron arms, and can be reversed to suit the direction the car may be moving. The *American Railway Journal* characterizes the Baltimore and Ohio as the Railroad University of the United States, saying that "its reports have in truth gone forth as

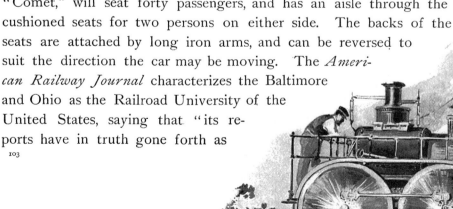

"Forrest State"
1853

a text-book, and the road and its workshops have been a lecture-room to thousands who are now practicing and improving upon their experience." Phineas Davis, the builder of the " York," the first and of nearly all the succeeding locomotives on the road, is dead, having been run down and killed by one of his own engines. Gillingham, the Superintendent of Machinery of the line, and Ross Winans, his assistant, resign, and take the Company's shops at Mount Clare, under contract to supply the road with locomotives at a stipulated price, and to give precedence to the Company's work.

The brake invented by Evan Thomas, and in use on the Baltimore and Ohio, is found far superior to any preceding it. A horizontal iron shaft with a lever extends down from the center, and has two projecting lips near each end. This shaft is carried in iron brackets secured to the frame of the car on each side midway between the two axles of one of the trucks. A chain is attached to the lower end of the lever and extends to the platform of the car, where the brakeman is stationed. The brake-shoes, two segments of a circle corresponding to the curvature of the wheels, are constructed of wood and affixed to iron plates. These are suspended between the wheels, one block being on each side of the shaft and bearing against the projecting lips. When the brake is to be applied the chain is hauled forward, and the lever which stood vertical is drawn into a horizontal position, revolving the shaft and forcing the lips on the shaft against the brake-shoes, which are in turn forced against and stop the wheels.

Immediately following the opening of the Baltimore and Ohio to Washington, Postmaster-General Kendall recommends the transfer of the contract for carrying the mails between Washington and Baltimore, and Baltimore and Harper's Ferry, Frederick, and other points reached direct by the road, from the stage companies to the Railroad Company, and the order, the first of the character in the history of the United States, is issued. An arrangement has also been entered into between the Government and the Baltimore and Ohio Company, whereby the first mail-car in the country is run between Washington and Baltimore. One end of a baggage-car has been boarded up, and entrance to this space, which is reserved exclusively for the mail, is confined to the post-masters of the two

Manchester "Pioneer" 1855

Great Southern of Ireland 1854

cities, they holding the only keys. Further improvements, which embody the beginning of a mail-car system in the United States, have been perfected by the enlargement of the space in the car, and providing facilities for distributing the local mail en route.

1835 "Twin cars," as they are called, have been placed in service on the Philadelphia and Germantown road. They are constituted of two four-wheel cars joined together, leaving a door at the end of each and a passage through the center. There are two of these cars, the "Victoria" and the "President." Each have a bar-room at one end and a ladies' saloon at the other, the intervening space being fitted up with cushioned seats which extend along the sides as well as through the middle of the cars.

The prevailing English railway coach is one of three compartments, the center one covered and for first-class passengers, the other two without roof and for second-class passengers. On the Liverpool and Manchester road the "buffing apparatus," as it is termed, consisting of a series of rods and levers acting on springs similar to the elliptical carriage springs, which has been used to lessen the concussion when stopping, and creating much trouble through giving the cars a swinging lateral motion, is being superseded by a new contrivance of Bergin's. This is a combination of coiled springs with rods from end to end of the car, and is much more effectual in preventing the concussions in stopping or starting. The Boston and Lowell road is opened between the two cities, and is twenty-six and a third miles in length. Stephenson's "Rocket," the winner in the Rainhill competition of 1829, has been remodeled by changing the cylinders from an inclined to a nearly horizontal position, and the engine put in service on a coal road.

John Day has brought out the first solid wrought-iron locomotive wheel in England, and is also the inventor of the mode of cutting off the ends of railway bars by sawing them at a high heat with a rapidly revolving disk of iron, which reduces the price of rails thirty shillings a ton. Lemaire, of Brussels, is experimenting with a locomotive propelled by magnetic force, and it is said a successful trial has been made. The first locomotive by Garrett and Eastwick, built for the Beaver Meadow line in Pennsylvania, from the drawings of Joseph Harrison, Jr., who previously was for two years with Long and Norris, has been named

after the President of the road, "Samuel D. Ingham." It has outside cylinder connections, running gear after the Baldwin type, with one pair of wheels, the drivers, in the rear of the fire-box and a four-wheel truck in front. It has the dome or "Bury" boiler, but its distinguishing feature is Eastwick's new mode of reversing, consisting of the introduction of a movable block or slide, called a reversing valve, between the usual slide valve and the cylinder face. The "Ingham" has the rear platform covered with a roof, an innovation enginemen and firemen will hail with pleasure, as for the first time there is a recognition that they should be taken in out of the wet, as the saying goes. Samuel B. Dougherty, so long with William T. James, is now with Dunham, a builder of locomotives in New York, the heavier parts of which, such as the cranks, driving wheels, shafts, etc., are ordered from England by Robert S. Stevens, the putting together and the lighter work only being done by Dunham. These engines are of the Stephenson's "Mercury" type. Dunham has, however, built a distinctively American engine for the Engineer Transportation Company. It has one pair of drivers, a four-wheel truck and four eccentrics on the driving axles.

On the retirement of Colonel Long from the firm of Long and Norris, 1836 William Norris succeeds to the business, and in 1836 in his very first locomotive, accomplishes results so unprecedented as to arouse the whole engineering world. The "George Washington" is on six wheels, the drivers, of which there is one pair, are four feet in diameter, located forward of the fire-box, and in front of them there is a vibrating four-wheel truck. The cylinders are outside. The "Washington" weighs fourteen thousand four hundred pounds,

and a very large proportion of the entire weight rests upon the driving wheels. Placed upon the Columbia road this engine performs the supposed impossible feat of drawing a load of nineteen thousand two hundred pounds at a speed of fifteen miles per hour up the inclined plane at Peter's Island, which is two thousand eight hundred feet long, with a rise of one foot in fourteen. The action of the draft link connecting the tender with the engine results in practically throwing all the weight but that of the forward truck frame and wheels, directly upon the driving wheels. This gives an adhesion not far from one-third the weight on the driving wheels, and the feat referred to is so amazing an achievement that it is deemed by many who were not present at the trial as absolutely incredible.

James Brooks, of Philadelphia, has built a locomotive for Henry R. Campbell, of the same city, which introduces an entirely new and distinctive type, and is the first American eight-wheel passenger-engine. The four driving wheels, all coupled, are placed one pair behind and one pair in front of the firebox, the remaining four wheels being in a swiveling truck forward. The striking feature of its performance is that it proves the possibility of running locomotives over grades of a hundred or more feet to the mile, without the use of planes or the building of tunnels. Baldwin is displacing the single eccentrics on his engines, and introducing instead double eccentrics with hooks in the place of links.

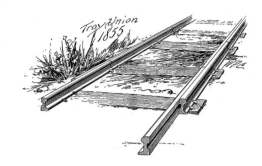

Tayleur has completed the "Star," for the Liverpool and Manchester, the first of an order for ten short-stroke passenger-engines. The cylinders are fourteen inches in diameter and have a stroke of only twelve inches. In the "Londoner" Harrison, in England, has made an effort to increase speed by spur gearing, the ratio of the gearing being three to one. The driving wheels of this engine are four in number, and six feet in diameter, the coupling being vertical, that is—one wheel directly above instead of following the other. The cylinders are sixteen by twenty inches, the boiler is upon one carriage and the engine on another, and the steam is conveyed from the boiler to the engine through a jointed pipe. The boiler is forty-four inches in diameter, and eight feet seven inches long, the firebox unusually large and the grate area over seventeen square feet. The cost of locomotive power for the hauling of trains on the Liverpool and Manchester for 1836 is at the rate of $7,000 a mile or $210,000 for the thirty miles, and the entire operating expenses $20,000 a day. The standing order as to gauges of railways in England has been suspended, and the new lines can be of any gauge desired. George Stephenson has patented a wheel with a cast-iron nave and rim,

and hollow wrought-iron or gun-barreled spokes. The two engines, the "Andrew Jackson" and the "John Hancock," recently made by Gillingham and Winans for the Baltimore and Ohio, show a tractive power with a weight of

107

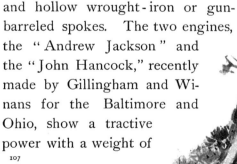

eight tons much exceeding the greatest that has up to this time been obtained on the Liverpool and Manchester with engines weighing twelve tons. The passenger car " Victory," built by Imlay, is the first with a raised roof, that is to say with deck lights, as they are termed. Its form is that of a coach body between the trucks, and a compartment over one truck is used for toilet purposes and one over the other for a bar. The Baltimore and Ohio bridge spanning the Potomac at Harper's Ferry is finished, and a connection thus established with the Winchester railroad. The Utica and Schenectady road is opened for business, the entire length of seventy-eight miles. Alabama has sixty-two miles of road under construction ; Delaware seventeen miles finished ; Georgia, twelve miles ; Kentucky eighty-five miles ; Louisiana, five miles ; Maryland, one hundred and forty-four completed and seventy under construction ; Massachusetts, seventy-two miles ; Mississippi, twenty-six miles ; New Jersey, one hundred and five miles ; New York seventy miles finished and two hundred under construction ; Pennsylvania three hundred and ninety-two completed, and two hundred and thirty-four in progress ; Rhode Island, forty-six in progress ; South Carolina, one hundred and thirty-six miles finished ; Virginia, one hundred and ninety-five miles completed, and eighty-six under construction.

There are stage connections between Chicago and the East, although they are not always to be relied upon for first-class accommodations. The Great Eastern mail stage is sometimes such in fact, that is an actual coach, but is as often merely a wagon with a canvas cover.

There is much agitation in London of the question of passing through tunnels on railways, of the harmful effects particularly upon the aged and infirm, it being brought about by the opening of the tunnel at Liverpool. It is a mile and a third in length, twenty-one feet high, the span of the arch twenty-five feet, and from one end to the other is cut through solid rock. An arrangement has been perfected on the Cumber- land Valley road to accommodate passengers who travel at night, and at the close of 1836 the first sleeping-car be- comes of record. Four sections of a car are fitted up so as to form beds or rather places to stretch out upon, for there are no bedclothes, excepting a pillow and thin mat- tress to each shelf, for that is about what it is. Chilled wheels have been introduced for cars and trucks.

Hogarth
1856

Barlow's Saddle Back
1856

The "Mazeppa," Winans' new type of locomotive, wherein he has transformed the "grasshopper" to the "crab," is on the Baltimore and Ohio. The upright boiler of the "grasshopper" is retained, but set lower, the centre of gravity of the whole machine being dropped down one foot. The cylinders are placed horizontally instead of vertically, as in the "grasshopper" type of engines, and attached to the back end of the frame, giving the locomotive the appearance of moving backward instead of forward, hence the nomenclature—the "Crab." There are four three-foot wheels, and the axles are but four feet from center to center. The "Mazeppa" weighs twelve tons, while the "grasshoppers" weigh but ten.

1837   The Baltimore and Ohio Company, greatly impressed with the wonderful performance of Norris's "Washington" on the Columbia road, orders one of the same type with improvements. This engine, the "La Fayette," is delivered in 1837. It is the first six-wheel locomotive on the road, and has a pair of drivers in front of the smoke-box, and a four-wheel swiveling leading truck. The boiler is horizontal, multitubular, with a dome fire-box. There are two double-acting cylinders, placed on the outside of the smoke-box, the piston rods extending through the back head to cross heads, and the connecting-rods are attached to crank-pins in the driving wheels. Each valve is worked by two eccentrics on the driving shaft, with drop-hook eccentric rod, which may be lifted on and off the pins on a rock shaft by cams operated by a lever on the foot-plate. There is one pump on the right hand side. The results obtained from this locomotive have already been so very satisfactory—her adhesion being remarkable and her power on grades so far beyond all previous experience, that the Company is negotiating with Norris for several others. Baldwin has introduced another innovation in the shape of iron instead of wood for the frames of his engines. The "Hercules," just finished by Garrett, Eastwick and Harrison, marks an epoch in American construction. In it the designer, Joseph Harrison, Jr., has so perfected his plans that an entire absence of equalizing beams between the drivers, and nothing but the ordinary steel springs over each journal to equalize the weight upon them, is no longer a feature of the American type of locomotive. As a matter of fact this is, however, still the style of English and all European engines, the equalizing beams of Harrison being the first in the world, and the "Hercules" is therefore a

radical departure from anything hitherto known anywhere. The engine has eight wheels, Harrison in this having followed the plan of the "Campbell," the want of flexibility in latter, the first of the eight wheelers, having shown the enormity of this defect as well as the importance of having a better distribution of weight upon the rails, and a locomotive for freight purposes much heavier than has yet been used. The purpose as a whole is accomplished by the introduction of Eastwick's plan of a separate frame under the rear end of the main frame, with two axles in the former, one pair in front of and the other behind the fire-box. This separate frame is made rigid and vibrates upon its center vertically. It is held together firmly at the ends, both sides at all times moving in the same plane, but it thus overcomes the undulation of the track in a perfect manner only when the irregu larities are alike on both rails. The weight of the engine rests upon the center of the sides of this separate frame through the intervention of strong springs which are above the main frame, the separate frame being held in place by a pedestal billeted to the main frame, the center of the separate frame vibrating upon a journal sliding vertically in this pedestal. In the "Hercules" is intro duced for the first time in steam machinery the bolted stub instead of the gib and key, for holding the strap on the connecting-rods. The engine has cylinders twelve by eighteen inches, and the reversing, instead of being accomplished through the eccentric or valve block, is performed by a plate between the valve and its seat, by a movement of which the steam-ports may be brought into com munication with either end of the cylinder. The boiler is horizontal, multitubu lar, with a dome or "Bury" fire-box, and the engine complete weighs fifteen tons. Doubts which have been expressed as to a road with a flat rail, five-eighths of an inch thick and two and a half inches wide, laid upon wooden string-pieces with mud sills underneath, supporting a fifteen-ton locomotive such as the Hercules, have been demonstrated to be groundless by the performance of the engine itself, on the Beaver Meadow line for which it was built.

The Hawthornes in England have constructed for the Great Western Rail way, from designs by Thomas Harrison, two locomotives with the engines upon a frame separate from the fire-box and boiler. The "Hurricane," one of these engines, has a pair of driving wheels ten feet in diameter, the largest ever made. The "Thunderer," the other engine, has sixteen-inch cylinders, with twenty-inch stroke, four coupled driving wheels, six feet in diameter, and geared three to one, in order to be equal to a wheel eighteen feet in diameter. In Hackworth's "Arrow," for the Stockton and Darlington, the cylinders are twenty inches in

diameter, and the stroke but nine inches. The "Swift," built for the same line by the Hawthornes, is a four-wheel engine with vertical cylinders, the connecting-rods working down to an intermediate shaft, coupled at each side to the crank-pins by coupling rods. Church's "Eclipse" has two steam domes, and a single pair of driving wheels six feet two and a half inches in diameter, placed under the middle of the boiler. The horizontal outside cylinders, eleven and a quarter inches in diameter, with twenty-four inch stroke, are located behind the fire-box. The "Eclipse" is a tank engine, weighing fourteen tons, two-thirds of the weight being on the drivers. The "Ajax," built by the Haigh Foundry, for the Leicester and Swannington road, has cylinders fourteen by eighteen inches, four coupled wheels four and a half feet in diameter, and boiler tubes two and a quarter inches in diameter, instead of one and five-eighths, which is the general practice. Thomas Rogers, who has started in on locomotive construction in his shops at Paterson, New Jersey, has progressed so far that the order of the New Jersey Railroad and Transportation Company, for an engine, is about filled. Meantime the President of the Mad River and Lake Erie Railroad Company, which is, as yet, practically no more than on paper, not a foot of the road being in existence, visits Paterson, sees the locomotive nearly completed, and determines to purchase it. No use for Rogers to say that it is for another company; the Westerner declares that a duplicate can be built for the New Jersey people, and Ohio will have the engine whether or no, and its name shall be the "Sandusky." And "Sandusky" it is, being the first locomotive west of the Ohio River. It is on six wheels, four in the forward truck, and one pair, the driving wheels, on the outside. In this engine are introduced, for the first time in locomotive practice, four fixed eccentrics and counterbalance weights in the wheels. The "Sandusky" has a horizontal boiler, multitubular, and a steam dome. There are two horizontal cylinders, located outside of the smoke-box and coupled to cranks inside of the driving wheels. The frames are outside of the wheels, and the eccentrics are on the driving axle outside of the frames, with eccentric rods

reaching backward to a rock shaft, with which they can be connected or disconnected at will by a lever on the foot-plate of the engine. The engine is taken to Ohio by water, and produces such an impression that the State Legislature by formal enact-

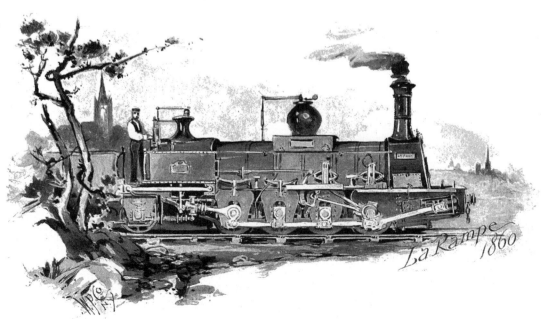

ment makes its gauge the standard for all railroad lines building within the commonwealth.

In New England, Griggs, of the Boston and Providence, seats his engine tires on wood. The driving wheels are of cast iron and have a series of dove-tailed grooves across the width in which oak blocks are inserted. The tire is then placed directly upon the wood while hot, and quenched in water the moment it is in place, to prevent charring the oak setting. No tire bolts are employed. Griggs has also introduced counter-weights in his driving wheels. In England the Hawthornes are the first to employ four fixed eccentrics and lap on the valves, and Roberts and Braithwaite the first to introduce counter-weights in driving wheels.

The New Castle and Frenchtown road, in Delaware, has a system of signalling which is giving satisfaction. A line of cedar poles have been put up and provided with cleats a foot apart which enable the station men to climb them, and with spy-glasses sight the succeeding stations in either direction. As a train approaches, if all is well, a flag is waved ; if no train is in sight anywhere, a big ball is displayed, which means an accident or delay. In this way an understanding is conveyed along the entire line of what to expect, and employees and patrons govern them-selves accordingly. A charter has been obtained from the Illinois Legislature for the Galena and Chicago Union Railway, the project contemplating a line from Chicago to the Mississippi.

In Belgium the railway line from Termonde to Ghent is opened, the celebra-tion of the event taking place in September, when five locomotives draw a hundred coaches filled with people. In Scotland the experiment has been tried of building a section of railway on a canal tow-path, and pulling the boats with a locomotive engine. 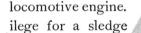 In Russia, the Emperor has granted a ten-year priv-ilege for a sledge road, as it is denominated. It consists of affixing the wheels to the railroad instead of to the coaches, and drawing or moving a sled-like platform upon the wheels, instead of the wheels on the rails as in the ordinary way.

The gauge of the Great Western Railway in England has been made seven feet between the rails, and several lines in Scotland have five feet six inches gauge. The width

Haswell's "Duplex" 1861

between the double tracks on the Liverpool and Manchester is the same as between the rails, four feet eight and a half inches. On the London and Birmingham and the Grand Junction Railway it is six feet. On several of the English lines, the roadway on either side of the track is raised about two feet high, as an additional precaution against trains going over embankments. The railroad in Cuba, eighty miles in length, from Havana to the Port of Batabano, is now open for business for fifty miles south of Havana, the locomotive used being a very heavy and powerful one, built by the Braithwaites, of London. The line in Russia between St. Petersburg and Zarskojeselo is completed, and Hackworth has shipped to the order of the Emperor a specially constructed locomotive of unusually large dimensions, which on preliminary trials has attained a speed exceeding seventy miles an hour. The Birmingham Railway in England announces that it will require two million pounds more than the estimate to finish the road. On the railway between Prague and Piken, in Germany, which is nearing completion, the work is being done very largely by females, and the pay equal to about sixpence a day, English money. Upwards of two thousand German women are regularly engaged as laborers in forming embankments, making open cuts and the like. In two years on the line equal to forty English miles, seven hundred thousand cubic yards of excavation, over eight hundred thousand cubic yards of embankment, and the laying of the way with malleable rails have all been done by these women laborers, and this together with seventy-three bridges, each from three to eighteen yards in length, one hundred and thirty-three culverts, and two hundred and thirty-six wagons, have only cost in the aggregate seventy-five thousand pounds.

The rails used on the German lines, like those in America in 1837, are of wood with iron plates, two and a half inches wide, and one inch thick on top. The wooden stringers so plated rest upon wooden sleepers, eight inches square, which in turn are placed in trenches on a foundation of broken stone.

The Baldwin engine of 1837 has a dome boiler, with the cylinders outside of and fastened to the smoke-box as well as the frame. The driving wheels are behind the fire-box. The framing is of iron, or of wood covered with iron plates, and is outside of the wheels, the driving wheels having two outside bearings, while the cylinders are so placed as to give an inside connection to the

crank. The crank is formed in the driving axle, but instead of being a complete double or full crank, the pin is extended through and keyed in the driving wheels. Each wheel is carried by an independent short axle, extending through to a bearing on the inside. This simplifies by more than one-half the making of the crankshaft, and at the same time increases its strength, and brings the thrust of the cylinders close to the wheels. The guide-bar for the cross-head, which has a double V top and bottom, is surrounded by the cross-head, and being hollow is made to serve the purpose of a boiler feed-pump.

Daniel Gooch, the new locomotive superintendent of the Great Western Railway of England, has had built from his designs engines with driving wheels of six, seven, and even eight feet diameter. The first delivered is the "North Star," constructed by the Stephensons, and her trial trip made on New Year's Day, 1838. She has cylinders sixteen by eighteen inches, and driving wheels seven feet in diameter, the gauge being seven feet. The "Æolus," built by Tayleur for the same line from plans by Gooch, has drivers eight feet in diameter.

It has been decided to lay a fifty-two pound edge rail on wooden cross ties on the extension of the Baltimore and Ohio west of Harper's Ferry, and several portions of the old line will at once be relaid with rails of this character and weight. Four additional engines, built for the road by Norris, have been delivered. The first of these, the "Philip E. Thomas," has four driving wheels, all connected, and four truck wheels, one pair having solid plates and the other spokes. Her cylinders, placed outside on the smoke-box and on an incline, are twelve inches in diameter with an eighteen-inch stroke. The boiler is horizontal, with a dome fire-box.

In the Baltimore *Chronicle* of October 31 this announcement appears: "The cars intended for night traveling between this city and Philadelphia, and which afford berths for twenty-four persons in each, will be placed on the road and used for the first time to-night."

In Kentucky two-story cars have been introduced on the Lexington and Ohio road. The lower story is enclosed and reserved for the use of ladies and children, and the upper open and intended for men. Rogers has delivered the "Arreseoh," which is his second engine, to the New Jersey Railroad and Transportation Company. Swinburn made the drawings for it

114

as well as for the "Sandusky." The new locomotive is considerably heavier than the first one, but otherwise is similar.

The "Samson," built by Hackworth, and the first locomotive in Nova Scotia, is a six-wheeler, with all wheels coupled. The boiler is horizontal and has return tubes, the fire-box and smoke-stack being at the same end. The cylinders are double acting, located vertically above the back pair of driving wheels, and secured to the boiler. The piston-rods extend through the lower heads of the cylinders, and connect with a system of levers giving a parallel motion, and the connecting-rods are attached to the back drivers. The valves are worked by four eccentrics, two for each valve, placed on the back axle. The valve arrangement is very complicated and located in a recess in the back end of the boiler. At the front end of the engine an iron basket is hung, in which to burn fagots to light the way at night. The first locomotive built by French engineers with French iron has been tested on the St. Cloud and Paris Railroad. It ran from Paris to St. Cloud in sixteen minutes, and back in thirteen and a half, equal to about thirty-three miles an hour. Many of the English engines built for the Continental railways have six-foot driving wheels. Worsdell, in England, suggests a mail crane, and takes out a patent on this method of handling the mail at way stations without stopping or retarding the speed of trains. Iron tubes are being laid on the line of the Great Western Railway, in which wires are placed for establishing communication between the various stations by means of Wheatstone's electrical telegraph. The cost is about a hundred pounds per mile. Samuel Dougherty, since his service with Dunham in New York, has taken locomotives to Natchez, to New Orleans, to the Buffalo and Niagara Falls road, and two, the "Harlem" and the "New York," to the Harlem Railroad, and has returned to his old position as foreman with William T. James, who has just turned out the "Brother Jonathan" for the Harlem road. This engine has a horizontal tubular boiler, and cylinders eight inches in diameter with a twenty-four inch stroke, one pair of four-foot drivers, a four-wheel truck, and a most peculiar valve gear operated without eccentrics. No slide valves are used, the steam admission and exhaust being controlled by a hollow steam-pipe, extending the whole length of the boiler, in place of the usual dry pipe. This pipe re-volves, and has four steam openings at its smoke-box end, one for each end of

each cylinder, and out on an angle, so that by adjusting a central pipe a cut-off is formed. Although a good deal like a gun without lock, stock, or barrel, as compared to the usual fowling iron, this locomotive, nevertheless, does fairly well. Dougherty leaves James, enters the service of the Harlem road, and becomes the engineer of the " Brother Jonathan," with which the road is opened to White Plains. The number one locomotive of the Philadelphia and Reading, the "Rocket," built by Braithwaite, of England, has been received. She is on four wheels, the rear pair of which are the drivers. The boiler is horizontal, multitubular, with dome fire-box. The cylinders are under the smoke-box, slightly inclined, the rear ends being the highest. The piston-rods extend through the back-heads of the cylinders to the cross-heads, and the cranks are formed on the back axle. The valves are in steam chests over the cylinders, and are each operated by two eccentrics on the crank axle, with eccentric rods extending forward through an opening in the smoke-box to a rock shaft forward of the cylinders. A shaft operated by a lever on the foot-plate has upright links connected to the eccentric rods, one rod of each pair being coupled ahead of the rock-shaft pin, and the other back, so that as the lever at the foot plate is moved either forward or backward, one eccentric rod is engaged and the other disengaged. A pump is worked from each cross-head. In the engines now built by Eastwick and Harrison the effects of the rigidity of the separate frames of the "Hercules" in passing over varying inequalities of the track on one side or the other are obviated by an improvement of Harrison's, consisting of placing the driving-axle bearings in pedestals bolted to the main frame and by the use of a compensating lever above vibrating on its center at the point of attachment to the main frame. The ends of this lever rest on the axle boxes through a pin passing through the frame. These levers vibrate on each side of the engine separately, and leave all the unevenness in both rails within a prescribed limit, which is governed by the play of the axle boxes in the pedestals.

In 1839 Isaac Hinkley, of Boston, produces his first loco- 1839 motive, the " Lion," which is on four wheels, all drivers. The frame is outside of the wheels, and the cylinders are outside connected, being secured to the smoke-box on an incline. The boiler is horizontal, with the fire-box overhanging the rear wheels. Norris delivers to the

Baltimore and Ohio the "Arrow," which has six wheels, and is the first on the line with crank axles and inside cylinders. She has five-foot drivers and cylinders twelve inches in diameter with a twenty-four-inch stroke. The "Arrow" is making a great record for speed in carrying Presidential messages from Washington, and is regarded as the fastest engine in the country. A gradient of three-quarters of a mile, rising at the rate of one hundred and fifty-four feet to the mile, on the Hudson and Berkshire road is worked regularly by a Norris locomotive. The railroad from Amsterdam to Rotterdam, the first in Holland, is opened from Amsterdam to Haarlem. Eastwick and Harrison have completed the locomotive "Gowan and Marx" for the Philadelphia and Reading Railroad, under the stipulation that of the whole weight of eleven tons nine shall rest on four driving wheels and that anthracite coal shall be burned in a horizontal boiler. To distribute the weight on the drivers as exacted, the rear axle is placed under the fire-box somewhat in advance of its central line instead of behind the box as in the "Hercules." The boiler is of the "Bury" type, and the fire-box has the unprecedented length of five feet. The number of tubes used is largely in excess of the usual quota, and they are two inches in diameter, and but five feet long, filling the cylindrical part of the boiler almost to the top. The cylinders are twelve and a half by eighteen inches, and the steam is admitted throughout the full stroke. The driving wheels are forty-two inches. The Gurney draft-box is used, with a number of exhaust jets employed to excite the fire when the engine is standing as well as when in motion. The tractive power of this locomotive in proportion to its length is notable, and its performance causes extended remark abroad as well as at home. Sterling, of Dundee, Scotland, has built three locomotives, the "Britannia," "Victoria," and "Caledonia," for the Arbroath and Forfar Railway, which are the first in Europe to combine inside bearings with outside cylinders and six wheels. Gray, of the Liverpool and Manchester road, employs the variable blast-pipe in the "Cyclops" to regulate the activity of the fire, according to the work done by the engine. Six locomotives constructed from Gray's drawings for the Hull and Selby line also have the variable blast-pipe.

A Baldwin engine on the Reading road is officially reported as having drawn from Reading to Norristown—forty-

one miles—forty-five cars loaded with one hundred and fifty tons of rails and iron, making in all two hundred and twenty-one tons behind the tender, in three hours and forty-one minutes running time. The "Albion" is the second locomotive sent by Hackworth to Nova Scotia, and has six wheels, all coupled. The boiler, which is horizontal and multitubular, has a circular fire-box in the waist. The "Hector," constructed for the Leicester and Swannington road in England, is a six-wheeled coupled freight engine, having cylinders sixteen by twenty inches, and wheels four feet six inches in diameter. The boiler is jacketed with sheet-iron plates instead of polished wood, as is the prevalent custom. One pair of the driving wheels is without flanges. This locomotive is constructed to work with a steam pressure of one hundred and twenty pounds—a bold departure in England — but in a vase-looking arrangement upon the boiler is a locked safety-valve, set to blow off at ninety pounds.

Early in 1840 Norris delivers the "Philadelphia," "Columbia," "Atlantic," 1840 and "England," four of eight locomotives ordered by the Birmingham and Gloucester Railway, in England. The design followed in the construction of these engines is that of the "Washington" and "La Fayette" on an enlarged scale. The "Philadelphia," which has cylinders ten and a half by eighteen inches, driving wheels four feet, weight of engine in working order nine and a half tons, is selected as the trial engine for the great test of climbing the Lickey incline plane which has always been worked by machinery. This grade is two miles in length, and the inclination one in thirty-seven. No thought was entertained in England that a locomotive could be worked upon it to any advantage whatever, until the surprising record made by the Norris engine, "George Washington," on the Columbia road at Philadelphia, this leading to the first order ever given by an English road to an American builder. The "Philadelphia" surmounts the inclined plane without difficulty, and so greatly are the stipulations of the company exceeded, that Norris is at once given his second English order, this time for sixteen locomotives of the same type as the others.

Bury, the English locomotive builder, declares in a letter to the directors of the road that he can accomplish with his engines whatsoever American engines can, and sends one of a special type to prove it. He fails, however, as his locomotive comes to a stand-still before getting half-way up the incline. The company abandons the use of fixed power on the incline, thus reducing operating expenses to such an extent that the shares of stock have advanced five pounds, or nearly twenty-five dollars, each.

Allan, on the Grand Junction road, in England, has changed the "Æolus," "Tartarus," and "Sunbeam" from inside to outside cylinder engines. New coaches on the York and North Midland Railway have seats through the centre, but no windows except those in the upper part of the doors, of which there are two, one on each side. The Liverpool and Birmingham passenger train consists of ten cars or carriages, drawn by a ten-ton locomotive with outside cylinders. Great changes are taking place on the American lines as regards the roadway, the H, the T, and the latest, the U, rails supplanting the "snake-head" and others of the earlier forms. The weight per yard is largely increasing, and in many instances more than doubled. Cross-ties are also being put down to strengthen and make the track firmer and better. In a very few instances they are of iron, but as a rule are of wood.

On the New York and Erie, gradients rising at the rate of one in eighty feet for several miles in length are being worked by locomotives. A Norris engine on the Boston and Worcester road draws a load of one hundred and fifty-one tons, exclusive of the weight of thirty-seven cars and a tender, over grades thirty feet to the mile, an amazing achievement, all things considered. Another notable performance is that on the Reading road, of an Eastwick and Harrison engine, weighing eleven tons, which draws a gross weight of four hundred and twenty-three tons of twenty-two hundred and forty pounds each, fifty-four and a half miles in five and a half hours. John Brandt, of Lancaster, Pennsylvania, has introduced a new four-wheel locomotive of his make on the Reading, and the Winans' "crabs," of which there are four on the same road, are, to quote the men handling them, "pulling like elephants." The Boston and Worcester road has placed a light, with powerful reflectors, in front of a locomotive which is used on the line at night. There is on the Tioga road a car built by the Harlans, at Wilmington, Delaware, which is thirty-six feet long, eight feet high, and six feet wide. The body is supported on rubbers in the pedestals,

Mitchell's "Consolidation" 1866

the wheels are outside of the bearings, and the car is fitted with draw-bar and chain brakes. Ventilation is obtained by means of a ten-inch flue in the center, and light is furnished by two candles, one at each end of the car. The windows do not raise, but there are panels between them which do. There is an aisle down the center, and the seats placed across the car, have iron frames, are upholstered with leather, and will each accommodate two passengers. The car is named the "Tioga," and is one of several ordered from the same firm. On the South Carolina, or properly speaking the Charleston and Hamburg Railroad, a new passenger car has also been placed in service. This car is barrel-shaped, thirty feet in length in the clear, with a platform two and a half feet long at each end. It is named the "Jasper" and has two four-wheeled trucks. The framework consists of staves grooved and dovetailed together and supported by six iron hoops, two and a half inches wide by one-half an inch thick. The diameter at the center is nine feet, and at the ends eight feet. The staves are one and a quarter inch boards five to six inches wide, extending the whole length of the car. There are twenty glazed windows, fifteen by thirty inches, in each side, the sash being opened by pushing it up overhead. The seats are arranged longitudinally inside the car on either side. A freight car twenty-one feet long, built on the same principle, is likewise on the road.

The car seats in use, particularly on the American lines, have passed through an evolution embracing many stages, such, for instance, as simply wooden boards, then covered with oil-cloth, leather, carpet (first plain and then stuffed), cloth, cane split, tow stuffed, straw padded, etc., until the highest standard of the development is now reached on the Baltimore and Ohio in spring seats, with hair or plush covering and reversible backs.

The "Gowan and Marx," the Eastwick and Harrison engine, has so favorably impressed the Russian engineers, Melkikoff and Trafft—commissioned by Emperor Nicholas to examine the railroads and machinery in America and Europe — that they have reported in favor of the American system and the Eastwick and Harrison locomotives for the line from St. Petersburg to Moscow. Samuel Hall has applied his patent of 1841 for burning anthracite coal to the engine "Bee," on the Midland Railway, and it is the first successful plan for the use of such fuel in Great

Ramsbottom's "Smeaton" 1866

Britain. Crampton, in England, has built a locomotive especially for high speed, in which the center of gravity of the boiler is made considerably lower than the common practice, and an intermediate crank shaft without wheels is introduced and connects the moving parts. Stephenson's three-cylinder engine which he has patented, has two outside cylinders located midway on the frame, and from the third or middle cylinder the connecting-rod is passed by a partition from the fire-box to the driving-box in the rear. An English combination car, as it may be termed, for when not in use for third-class passengers it is employed for cattle, has a roof, but is sided or closed only about half way up.

John W. Garrett

1842   In 1842 the "Robert L. Stevens," a locomotive named from its designer, is planned with an additional pair of wheels, which Stevens calls connecting wheels, located directly on top of the two pairs of regular driving wheels, the periphery of each of the top wheels coming in contact with the periphery of two of the lower wheels. The Sharp-Roberts, an English engine, is a type used very much in France for passenger trains. It has a single pair of large drivers and two pair of carrying wheels, each pair moving independently of the other. The cylinders are at the bottom of the fire-box, between it and the driving wheels, the movement being communicated to the drivers through a crank axle.

Baldwin, in the "Thompson," a twelve-ton engine, has demonstrated that in the six-wheel connected locomotive, with flexible truck, the weight is distributed on six points, and therefore it can with safety be greatly increased. Baldwin has also perfected, in the "American," a plan for constructing heavy freight locomotives, so that the wheels of the leading trucks are converted into drivers without interfering with their other and common use. A number of Winans engines, of the "grasshopper" and the "crab" types, all of them burning anthracite coal, are in use on Eastern roads. The "Number 71" on the Midland Railway in England, built by the Stephensons, has been fitted up with the link motion, as perfected by William Howe, a mechanic in their employ,   and given her trial trip. The reversing lever rack has several   notches on either side of the center, and steam can be cut off at various proportions of the stroke from four and one-quarter to seventeen and one-eighth inches.

In the "Mercury," built by Eastwick and Harrison for the Baltimore and Ohio, is introduced for the first time a single long spring in the leading truck.

Decapod "The Bee"
1867

Each end of this spring rests on one of the journal boxes and carries one end of a wrought-iron bolster on its center. The record of the "Mercury," for her first year is the unparalleled one of thirty-seven thousand miles. She is exceptionally fast, frequently attaining a speed of a mile a minute with the average passenger train.

The "Carroll of Carrollton," Winans' new creation of 1843, is a striking 1843 engine, being the first in America with a single pair of driving wheels seven feet in diameter. Winans introduces a device in this engine whereby when a grade is reached the weight is shifted from the trucks and concentrated upon the driving wheels. The valve motion is most peculiar, and the stroke is no less than forty-eight inches. She has proved to be so fast that her speed cannot be fully tested on any line in the country. The trial trip on the Baltimore and Ohio's Washington branch, demonstrates that there is almost no limit to her speed, and the engine could not be fully let out for fear she would jump the track. The "Carroll" is now on the Boston and Worcester road, where she is scaring the natives, not to speak of her engineer and fireman, by terrific bursts of speed when now and then cautiously opened up.

John Stevens, of Hoboken, has also built an engine with driving wheels seven feet in diameter, in which all of the machinery is on top of the boiler, the fire-box is hung under the axle, and the forward truck has six wheels. Crampton, in England, has changed the position of the wheels on his new engines, placing the smaller or carrying wheels in front and the larger or driving wheels at the rear end, behind the fire-box. The cylinders are outside. The Grand Junction Railway Company has brought out at its own shops the "Crewe" type of locomotives, which have driving wheels five feet six inches and six feet in diameter, and outside cylinders fifteen by twenty inches. For the London and South Western Railway John Gooch has also adopted outside cylinders, some of his engines hav- 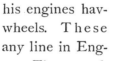 ing six-foot-six and others seven-foot driving wheels. These wheels are the largest in use at this time on any line in Eng- land, excepting those of seven-foot gauge. The total English railway mileage is now about eighteen hundred. Harrison, of Eastwick and Harrison, is in Russia, in response to the request of the Emperor, and in connection with Thomas Winans, of Baltimore, a contract has been closed with the Russian Government for one hun-

dred and sixty-two locomotives, and iron trucks for two thousand freight cars, all the work to be done in Russia in shops to be established there by the firm of Harrison, Winans and Eastwick.

1844 The first rail rolled in America is turned out in 1844 by a mill at Mount Savage, Allegheny County, Maryland, and the Franklin Institute, of Philadelphia, in honor of this event, has struck a silver medal. The rail is of the U form, and is laid on a longitudinal sill, to which it is fastened by an iron wedge, keyed under the sill, thus dispensing with outside fastenings. The rail weighs forty-two pounds, has been introduced on the line between Mount Savage and Cumberland, and also on the Baltimore and Ohio road. The mill has an order for rails weighing fifty-two pounds to the yard for the road from Fall River to Boston.

Ross Winans in the "Buffalo" has made another pronounced departure from conventional plans in locomotive construction, introducing in this engine the first eight coupled wheels in the world. The wheels are in two groups of four each, front and back of a vertical, multitubular boiler. There are two outside, horizontal cylinders on the frame above the driving wheels at one extreme end, with cross head, guide, and connecting-rod, the latter being attached to a cross shaft at the other end of the frame, the shaft having outside cranks at its ends and a central gear running into another upon one of the driving shafts. The Baltimore and Ohio does not own the "Buffalo," simply permitting it to be tested for some time on the road. It is the heaviest engine ever run over the line and is known as the "Mud Digger," because it pounds up so much dirt from the light track. The Baltimore and Ohio, however, has decided to have a number of locomotives with eight coupled wheels built by Winans and designed to burn Cumberland coal, but the boilers are to be horizontal and the weight more evenly distributed than in the "Buffalo."

In England Robert Stephenson, to overcome the speedy destruction of the chimneys and smoke-boxes in his locomotives, has patented what he terms the "long boiler," and in the first of this type just completed he has lengthened the tubes from nine to fourteen feet and placed all the axles under the barrel or circular part of the boiler. The driving wheels are between the front and rear carrying wheels, and the cylinders attached to the under side of the smoke-box.

In the "Champlain," built for the Reading road, Baldwin has introduced the cut-off valve, or as he terms it in 1845, the "half-stroke cut-off," instead 1845 of the two eccentrics, and it is known as the Baldwin "C" type of engine. It is also his first locomotive having four drivers and a four wheel truck. A similar engine of his is on the South Carolina road, having drivers five feet in diameter with springs between, arranged as equalizers. The cylinders are thirteen and three-quarters inches by eighteen, located inside the frames, but outside the smoke-box. The "Antelope," built by Hinkley, is on the Boston and Maine, and has driving wheels, six feet in diameter. Although an eight-wheel engine, the "Antelope" has but a single pair of drivers, there being a pair of small trailing wheels and a four-wheel truck. Her cylinders are eleven and a half by twenty-two inches. The "Bangor," on the same road, and also of Hinkley's make, has four drivers, coupled, five feet six inches in diameter. The "Robert Stephenson" is the model Stephenson engine of the year, being acknowledged the finest locomotive ever built at the Newcastle shops. All the mechanism for moving and reversing is underneath the boiler, the movement of the pump rods being obtained from the eccentrics. All six wheels are between the fire-box and the smoke-box, and the drivers are connected by outside rods to the forward pair of wheels. On the Great Western Railway, the "Ixion," having inside cylinders fifteen and three-quarters by eighteen inches, drivers seven feet in diameter, and four carrying wheels, has attained, on runs between London and Didcot, with an average load of sixty-six and a half tons, a maximum speed of sixty-two miles an hour. She has a record of fifty-three miles in one hour and eight minutes.

McConnell has designed and built for the London and North Western road the "Bloomer" type of engines, with inside frames and inside bearings only. Some of them have cylinders sixteen by twenty-two inches, and six-feet-six-inch or seven-foot drivers. McConnell is the first English designer to produce a locomotive able to surmount inclines. It is a tank engine for the Birmingham and Gloucester road, having six coupled wheels, three feet nine inches in diameter, cylinders eighteen by twenty-six, and a total weight of thirty tons. A committee of the House of Commons expresses the belief that there is at the present time ample evidence to justify the adoption of an atmospheric railway line. Commissioners appointed by royal command to inquire into the advisability of a standard or uniform gauge on English railways report unanimously in favor of such legislation as is necessary to establish it at four feet eight and one half inches. A return made to Parliament shows

124

that the projected railways, of which plans and sections have been deposited, as required by law, with the Railway Department of the Board of Trade, are in the aggregate equal to a distance twenty-four times that from one end to the other of the whole of England.

Griggs, of the Boston and Providence road, of New England, has put on that line an eight-wheel engine with inside cylinders, which is the first of this type having a swiveling truck. It is named the "Norfolk;" the cylinders are fourteen and a half by eighteen inches, and there are four coupled wheels four feet seven inches in diameter, and a four-wheel truck. The passenger trains in New York do not run after dark. Trains from Albany, westward, stop over night at Syracuse, while those from Buffalo for Albany stop over from supper to breakfast at Auburn. Two trains run each way daily, except Sunday, in summer, and one train in winter. The train leaving Buffalo in the morning reaches Rochester at one in the afternoon and Auburn at seven in the evening. On some of the Pennsylvania and Maryland lines there are cars having seats which can be converted into a fairly comfortable bed by turning them face to face and placing slats across as a support for a mattress.

James Brooks, in conjunction with Samuel Wright, has finished a locomotive in the former's shop in Philadelphia, in which the guides are cylindrical in form, bored out and arranged to serve the purpose of feed pumps, the cross head forming the piston of the pump. The valve gear is arranged so that when the engine is going forward the slide valve acts in the usual manner, and the reversing is done by a two-way cock which converts the exhaust-pipe into the steam-chest and the steam-chest into the exhaust-pipe.

The Baltimore and Ohio shops at Mount Clare have for some time been operated directly by the company, with James Murray as the superintendent. His first engine, and the first built by the company, the "Mount Clare," is on the road. The eight wheels upon which it is mounted are coupled by cranks outside of the frames, the wheels being in two groups of four each, front and back of a central cross shaft, having a crank at each end, to which the coupling or parallel rod is attached. The central shaft has a gear at its center above the central cross shaft, and parallel to it is a shorter shaft coming within the framing and suspended from the boiler. This shaft has a central gear running

into the one on the other shaft and cranks at the ends, to which the cylinders are coupled by means of connecting-rods. The two cylinders being located forward of the fire-box. The wheels are between the fire-box and the smoke-box, both of the latter overhanging. The boiler is of the horizontal, multitubular type. The valves are worked by two eccentrics, each on the upper short shaft, with hook ends on the eccentric rods, which engage pins on a rock shaft, and are thrown in and out of gear by a lever in the cab.

Gooch's "Great Western," on the railway after which it is named, is the European triumph of 1846, exciting English attention and admiration as no locomotive has ever done before. It has on several occasions started from Paddington and stopped at Didcot, fifty-three and a quarter miles in forty-seven minutes, and has obtained a maximum speed of seventy-eight miles an hour. The "Great Western," built expressly for the seven-foot gauge of road, has a single pair of driving wheels, eight feet in diameter, and without flanges. There are eight wheels in all, four forward arranged in a group but not in a "bogie" or flexible truck, and a pair of trailing wheels in the rear of the drivers. The cylinders are eighteen by twenty-four inches, and three hundred tubes in the boiler give nearly eighteen hundred feet of heating surface. Stephenson has added a pair of trailing wheels behind the fire-box on his "long boiler" locomotive, and it has thus become an eight-wheeler. In conjunction with Howe, he has completed two locomotives, each having three cylinders, two outside and one inside, in the belief that the alternate lifting on the opposite side of the engine will thus be counteracted.

Bridge rails are now rolled by the British Iron Company at Abersychan, thirty feet long and weighing ninety pounds to the yard. In the plan Crampton has patented in England to increase traction, he couples two ordinary engines together by their foot plates, beneath which he places the coke-boxes, while a tender for water occupies the position between the smoke-box end of one of the engines and the train.

Winans' "Delaware," for the Reading road, is his first perfected eight-wheel engine for burning anthracite coal, and with the introduction of it, and the "Maryland," on the line, the company's hitherto maintained practice of burning wood to bring coal to market is abandoned. Much difficulty has been experienced by the Reading people in securing a type of engine which will enable them to use their own fuel, anthracite coal, instead of wood, and Winans suc-

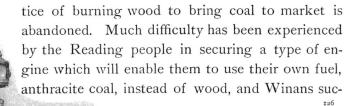

ceeds where many have failed. Originally these engines were on six wheels, all of them drivers, and forward of the fire-box. When the engine was placed on the road it was found that the excessive overhang threw too much weight on the back driving wheels, and a pair of twenty-four-inch wheels were therefore added between the rear of the fire-box and the pit of the tender. Weight is applied to them by a cylinder bolted to the fire-box and carrying boiler pressure. Thus, when the engine is running, the weight upon the rear driving wheels is reduced in accordance with the pressure upon the cylinder. Baldwin also has an eight-wheel connected engine on the Reading, his first of this type for freight service. Her cylinders are fifteen and a half by twenty inches, wheels forty-six inches in diameter, and weight forty tons. He is the first to introduce sand-boxes and has put a roof over the foot-board. Hitherto he has inclosed the foot-board with a railing only, but now it has a covering supported by four iron posts, and the engine men have added curtains, as a protection from the sun and rain.

Septimus Norris, a brother of William, has designed and completed for the Reading the first ten-wheel locomotive, the "Chesapeake," and it utilizes three-fourths instead of three-fifths of the whole weight for adhesion, while the gross weight is distributed upon ten points instead of upon eight, as in the eight-wheel engines. The "Chesapeake" has three pairs of drivers all connected, and a four-wheel truck forward; the drivers being forty-six inches in diameter, and the axles five inches in diameter. Her cylinders are fourteen and a half by twenty-two inches and weight twenty tons. The side rods are in two sections, entirely independent of each other, the main rod being connected to a main pin between them.

England has nineteen hundred miles of railway, of four feet eight and one-half inches, or narrow gauge, and two hundred and seventy-four miles of seven-foot or broad gauge. In Scotland all the gauge is four feet eight and one half inches. In Ireland it is five feet three inches. In France, four feet eight and one half, or the standard. In Belgium, the standard. Brunswick, Saxony, Austria, Bavaria, and Italy—all standard. In Holland it is six feet four, in Baden, five feet three inches, and in Strasburg six feet three inches.

Wright has designed and Brooks built a second locomotive, and in it the adhesion of the forward truck wheels is secured by a combination with a pair of driving wheels behind the fire-box. Increased heating surface is the purpose sought by the Lowell shops in the construction of the two engines, the "Baldwin" and the "Whistler," for the Boston and Lowell road. Both locomotives are the same, having a grate surface of eight square feet, fire-box heating surface of fifty-six square feet, one hundred and forty tubes eleven feet long and two inches in diameter, giving eight hundred and six square feet of tube heating surface. The engine has inside cylinders fifteen and one-half inches in diameter with an eighteen-inch stroke, four coupled drivers five feet six inches in diameter, and a forward truck.

Hinkley has completed the ten-wheeler "New Hampshire" for the Maine and Boston road. It has inside cylinders sixteen by twenty inches, six coupled wheels of forty-six inches diameter, while those in the four-wheel truck are thirty inches. George Escoll Sellers' new type of locomotive is for a middle rail track in Panama, and four have been constructed. They have the usual pair of cylinders working four coupled driving wheels on the level, while by means of an extra pair of cylinders and a corresponding pair of wheels working on vertical axles and gripping a middle rail, the steep inclines are surmounted. In the "Courier," Farley's engine for the Eastern Railroad in Massachusetts, the suspended link is introduced, and this form of valve is an innovation in New England. Francis, son of Richard Trevithick, has placed on the London and North Western road the pioneer locomotive with large boiler and high driving wheels on the four feet eight and one-half inch gauge, and the great controversy in England as to the comparative merits of this with the seven-foot gauge has received a new impetus, with the narrower in the lead. The "Cornwall" is the name of the engine, and in order to obtain a low center of gravity, Trevithick has placed the boiler under the driving axle. The drivers are eight feet six inches in diameter, the largest ever known on the gauge named. The engine has six wheels, one pair of trailers, outside connected cylinders seventeen and one-half by twenty-four inches, and on her trial trip reached a speed equal to seventy-nine miles an hour. Brunell's locomotive on the Great Western road has eight-foot driving wheels, and cylinders eighteen by twenty-four inches. In the Sharp engines, which are in such great favor in England, the dome is now placed so far forward as to be nearly against the chimney. In the Wilson's "Crampton" type of engine just finished for the Midland Railway there is a weight of eight tons to each wheel, the locomotive aggregating thirty-two tons, having but four wheels six feet six inches in diameter, and placed sixteen feet from center to center. With a light train she is very

"Mastodon" 1881

fast, exceeding, in spurts, seventy-five miles an hour. An engine of Crampton's design on the London and North Western, the "London," has a single pair of drivers eight feet in diameter, with cylinders eighteen by twenty inches. The "Courier," also after Crampton's plans, has a pair of seven-foot drivers behind the fire-box, while Allan, of the Crewe works, has likewise put seven-foot driving wheels in the "Velocipede."

1848 Nichols' locomotive, the "Novelty," on the Reading road, is attracting attention from the fact of its being upon two carriages, and in a certain way it is the talk of the early months of 1848. As a matter of fact the "Novelty" is a three-carriage affair, the engine being upon one, the boiler upon a second, and the tender constituting the third. The boiler is fourteen feet long and of a width equal to that of the frame of the carriage supporting it. The steam is carried through joint pipes to the engines, which are in front and on a separate truck or carriage. There are eight coupled drivers, each thirty-six inches in diameter, and the cylinders are eighteen by twenty inches. The weight of the forward or engine carriage, which is separate from the boiler, is twenty-one and a half tons. The "Novelty" burns anthracite coal, and her average speed is about ten miles an hour. Winans' first camel locomotive is on the Baltimore and Ohio, and in it he has introduced for the first time the cam cut-off instead of eccentrics. Other innovations are outside horizontal cylinders and coupling rods of flattened section with solid stub ends. There are eight coupled driving wheels forty-three inches in diameter, the wheel base being eleven feet three inches. A wide fire-box overhangs the back wheels, and there is a very large dome about midway of the boiler shell, the throttle being located in the dome at the back and operated by an eccentric and levers from a platform on the top of the boiler, the latter being almost entirely covered by the cab. In the fire-box there is a rocking grate worked by the fireman through levers from the tender. The frames are double slabs or plates, and are secured by thimbles or rivets. The valves are worked by two cams each, the rods have D hooks at the outer end, are weighted to hold them in place, and have a guard under the pins with which they engage. The pump is worked from the cross-head, and the valve stem and valve rod are coupled together. The cylinders are seventeen by twenty-

129

Baldwin's "Double Ender" 1882

two inches, the wheels are cast iron with steel tires, and only the two outer pairs are flanged. The grate is seven feet long and three feet six inches wide, and the engine complete weighs twenty-five tons.

Another eight-wheeled coupled locomotive on the Baltimore and Ohio is the "Dragon," one of four built expressly for the company by Baldwin, and the first in which that maker introduces the rocking grate. The engine is peculiar in that the four front wheels constitute a truck, although these wheels are of the same size as the four rear wheels—four feet—and all eight, as hitherto stated, are coupled. The two cylinders are attached to the sides of the smoke-box on a steep incline. The piston-rods extend through the back lower heads to the cross-heads. The connecting-rods are attached to the third pair of wheels, the back parallel rods being a continuation of the main·rod by means of a knuckle joint. The forward parallel rod is also in the same line, and the middle parallel rod takes hold of the outer end of the pin, while the main rod is bent to clear the second crank-pin and stub end. The valves are worked by two eccentrics each and a link.

Baldwin has constructed, something after the Adams practice in England, a very light engine for passenger service on the Vermont Central road. It is named the "Adams" and weighs but five tons. The cylinders are five and a half inches in diameter with a fourteen-inch stroke, and the driving wheels are four feet in diameter. Rogers' ten-wheelers on the six-foot gauge of the Erie road have nearly fifteen square feet of grate surface, seventy-two square feet of fire-box heating surface, one hundred and ninety-eight one and three-quarter inch tubes, thirteen feet long, presenting eleven hundred and twenty-seven feet of external service. These engines have cylinders eighteen by twenty inches, and five-foot driving wheels.

The rack rail has been adopted for the incline of one in seventeen on the Madison and Indianapolis road in Indiana, Baldwin having furnished two locomotives expressly for this incline, the "John Bright" and the "John Brough." The two Johns each have eight coupled wheels, four feet in diameter, and a pair of outside inclined cylinders, seventeen by twenty-two inches, for working these wheels only on the line where it is level, or nearly so. A rack rail laid midway between the ordinary rails, is ten inches wide, and the teeth have a pitch of four inches. The engine has a second pair of cylinders, seventeen by eighteen inches, placed vertically over the boiler at about the

Munich Compound 1884

middle of its length. The piston-rods work downward, and are connected to the axle of a stout pinion beneath the boiler. The pinion works into one of the driving wheels, which is about twice its diameter, has its axle supported in bearings in the lower ends of a pair of connecting-rods, and may be raised and lowered to engage the rack by a horizontal steam cylinder seven inches in diameter.

A large engine for the narrow or standard gauge, and intended by Crampton, its builder, to surpass the "Great Western" on the broad or seven-foot gauge, is in service on the London and North Western Railway. The "Liverpool," is the greatest locomotive for passenger traffic at this time, and settles the question of the feasibility of using the largest engines upon the four foot eight and one-half inch gauge. It has cylinders eighteen inches in diameter with a twenty-four-inch stroke, eight-foot driving wheels, and a boiler containing three hundred tubes two and three-sixteenths of an inch in diameter, and twelve feet three inches long. The total heating surface is two thousand two hundred and sixty square feet, the total wheel base eighteen feet, and the weight in working order thirty-five tons. Crampton, in altering one of the long-boiler engines on the Southeastern Railway by placing the driving wheels behind instead of in front of the fire-box, did all required to transform the locomotive to the Crampton type, the outside cylinders being already placed horizontally at some distance behind the smoke-box. The "Laublasch," another English engine, has two inside cylinders twenty by thirty inches. The outside rods are connected through double cranks to the crank-pins on the wheels, the lower crank to the forward, and the top crank to the back wheel, the crank axle being done away with entirely. The driving wheels are seven feet in diameter, and their two axles sustain the whole weight of the engine, which is said to have run at a speed of eighty-four miles an hour. Meyer, who gained his knowledge in practical locomotive construction from Norris while the latter was at the Royal Works in Austria, and who succeeded the American in charge of them, retains American ideas very largely in his present designs. For instance, the center-pin or pivot of the truck is placed near the leading axle, and the stroke of the plunger can be varied by means of a jointed lever working from a curved arm.

131

Van Borne's Compound 1886

The dimensions of the smoke-box are reduced by a plate or partition extending across it just above the top row of tubes, and the chimney extends downward to this partition.

Two bridges on the line of the Blackwall Railway in England are of peculiar form, and the first of their class erected for railway purposes. The roadway is supported by wrought-iron girders placed transversely between two arches or ribs constructed entirely of wrought iron. The clear span of one is one hundred and twenty feet, and of the other one hundred and sixteen feet. The latter bridge carries the railway over the Regent's Canal, and has each arch in the form of a box built of iron boiler plates eleven-sixteenths of an inch in thickness. A piece of naval architecture regarded as novel and extraordinary has had its engines fitted at Lancefield, England, and recently made an experimental trip down the river to Greenock and back. This vessel, which is built for the purpose of transporting railroad trains entire, is constructed of iron, and is one hundred and seventy-five feet long, thirty-four feet broad, and ten feet deep, the bottom being a very flat curve. Both ends are alike and quite square, so that they may be brought against the quay or wharf and the trains run on the deck from either end. The deck is flush and clear, fore and aft, and contains three lines of rails, which afford ample room for the longest train likely to require transportation.

The newest style of locomotive in England in 1849 is the " Jenny Lind," 1849 built by the Wilsons, of Leeds. She has outside frames and outside bearings for the leading and trailing wheels, but inside bearings for the driving axle. Her cylinders are fifteen by twenty inches, and wheels six feet in diameter. Timothy Hackworth, who for some years has not given much attention to locomotive construction, is again in the mechanical arena and with, as usual, a notable engine. It is on the York, Newcastle and Berwick line. The chief dimensions are : diameter of cylinders, fifteen inches ; stroke of pistons, twenty-two inches ; and diameter of driving wheels, of which there is a single pair, six feet. This en-gine has repeatedly run at the speed of seventy-five miles an hour, and is being prepared to make a regular run, with a light train, between York and Darlington, a distance of forty-five miles, in forty minutes. The success of this locomotive has led the builder's son, John W. Hackworth, to challenge Robert Stephenson to a con-

The Worsdell Compound 1887

test to prove to whom, as he says, the superiority in the construction and manufacture of locomotive engines now belongs. Crampton's locomotive for the Southeastern Railway, the "Folkstone," has inside cylinders, but with the driving wheels fixed to a straight axle. He employs a double crank shaft, also outside crank and coupling rod to communicate motion to the rear drivers, which are placed behind the fire-box. Adams's combination of locomotive and coach, for the Eastern Counties road, is constructed to accommodate eighty-four passengers. The wheel base is but twenty feet long, and the weight of the whole in working order fifteen tons seven hundred pounds. This is increased to about twenty-one tons by the weight of the passengers and luggage, the engine, coke, water, and passengers all being carried upon the same frame. Adams also has several carriages or coaches forty feet long and nine feet wide, which are supported on eight wheels, and will seat one hundred and sixteen passengers. One of these carriages attached to the "Enfield" offers accommodation for a total of one hundred and fifty passengers.

The "Dimpfel" water-tube boiler, introduced on express and other engines on the Philadelphia, Wilmington and Baltimore Railroad, has iron tubes of small diameter which open through the crown sheet of the fire-box, and being below it extend to and communicate with a water space at the fire-box end of the boiler. Although thus traversed by tubes, the whole length of the barrel of the boiler serves as a combustion chamber, the outlet for the products of combustion being at the bottom of the smoke-box. The "Fury," one of the three "Shanghais" built by Seth Wilmarth for the Boston and Worcester road, is an inside connected eight-wheel engine, with a short round truck. Her cylinders are fifteen by eighteen inches, the driving wheels sixty-six inches, and the boiler forty-eight inches in diameter. Rogers in introducing the link motion in his general practice has been so successful that it is already regarded as the dividing line between the present and the early and transitional stage of locomotive development. The "Victory" and the "Pacific" are his initial engines with this device. They have two six-foot driving wheels, a pair of thirty-three and one-half inch truck-wheels, and four thirty-three-inch wheels in the truck. The cylinders are sixteen inches in diameter with twenty-inch stroke. Baldwin, in abandoning the half crank, substitutes the outside connection therefor. In the

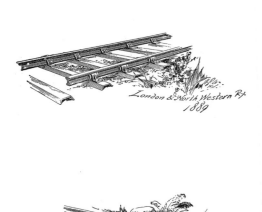

London & North Western Ry.
1889

Normantown Line
Queensland
1889

"Governor Paine," built by him for the Vermont Central Railway, the cylinders are seventeen inches in diameter with twenty-inch stroke, and the engine has a pair of six and one-half foot driving wheels. Three engines of the Crampton type are on the Pennsylvania Railroad, having been built by Baldwin. Seven engines constructed by Norris for the Camden and Amboy Railroad have each a single pair of eight-foot driving wheels, and a four-wheel truck, the cylinders being thirteen inches in diameter with a thirty-four-inch stroke. Norris, at the Schenectady shops, in the "Lightning," built for the Utica and Schenectady Railroad, follows the Crampton plan of placing the drivers back of the fire-box and adding extra carrying wheels. This engine has cylinders sixteen by twenty-two inches, and a single pair of drivers seven feet in diameter; the carrying wheels are four feet, and the front truck wheels three feet six inches in diameter. All these wheels are solid forgings, the first of this description. The "Lightning" has hauled a train of eight-wheeled cars at the rate of eighty miles an hour. It is becoming the practice to spread the axles of the truck wheels from the usual distance of three feet between centers to four feet six inches, and five feet, and in some cases six feet. The Amoskeag Company, in building the "Mameluke," has employed seven-foot coupled wheels, and cylinders fifteen inches in diameter with a twenty-four-inch stroke. The different railroad companies between Albany and Buffalo in New York have been consolidated under the general name of the New York Central, and the thin bar-iron rail has been replaced with a heavy uniform T rail throughout the entire system. The Michigan Central from Buffalo to Detroit is in operation. The Austrian Government, before commencing the construction of a railway over the Semmering Pass, sends a commissioner to America to investigate the subject of steep gradients, and he reports in favor of following the plan of the Baltimore and Ohio Railroad, which is to use continuous gradients not greater than one in forty-five.

Baldwin, in 1850, does away with the old form of dome boiler, substituting in its stead the wagon-top type. In his original engine Sellers placed his auxiliary driving wheels at the back of the loco-motive and conveyed motion to them from auxiliary en-gines through cranks and bevelled gear wheels. In his new engine, the "George E. Sellers," he transfers motion from the auxiliary engines to the crank shafts of the

134

Wolf-Compound 1889

auxiliary driving wheels, and also to the truck connections, with a separate shaft. Norris has sent seventeen engines to the Birmingham and Gloucester Railway in England, and no less than fifty-three to the Continent of Europe. Two outside cylinder engines of his make, with fourteen-inch cylinders and a thirty-two-inch stroke and coupled seven-foot driving wheels, are on the New York and Erie Railroad. The forty-two miles of the Galena and Chicago Union Railroad, from Chicago to Elgin, are completed. The population of Chicago at this time is twenty-eight thousand. The New York and Erie Railroad extends westward as far as Hornellsville, and the Western and Atlantic Railroad of Georgia is carried to the Tennessee River. The Michigan Southern, which was constructed by the State of Michigan, is in operation from Monroe to Hillsdale, a distance of sixty-nine miles, and has a wooden rail covered by a flat bar of iron.

There are now eight thousand six hundred miles of railroad finished and in operation in the United States, the total cost being $296,260,128.00. The greater portion of railroad construction has until quite recently been in the States bordering upon the Atlantic, and consists for the most part of isolated lines with a comparatively limited traffic, almost exclusively local. The internal commerce of the country is still largely conducted through water lines, natural and artificial, and over ordinary highways.

Midland R'y of England 1889

Six-wheel trucks for passenger-cars have become the rule rather than the exception. Telegraphic communication for railway operation is being generally established. In England, the "Bloomer" class of engines made for the London and North Western line is about the only departure this year from usual practice. They have sixteen-inch cylinders, a twenty-two-inch stroke, seven-foot driving wheels, and weigh twenty-eight and three-quarter tons. Tarpaulins have been superseded to a great extent on the Liverpool and Manchester road, for "goods" or freight traffic, by covered wagons or cars, from fourteen to sixteen feet long, with sliding doors and movable roofs, so that by means of a crane a bale of goods, however heavy, can be deposited in any part of the interior and be protected from damage by fire, wind, or rain. These covered cars weigh from four to five tons, and have a capacity of from six to eight tons.

The New York and Erie Railroad, from Piedmont to Lake Erie, a distance of four hun-

Salamon-Flaman 1890

dred and fifty-one miles, is opened in May, 1851. The Vermont Central is 1851 also completed and in operation, as is also the Western Railroad, extending from Boston to Albany, a distance of two hundred miles. The Galena and Chicago Union Railroad is completed to Freeport, one hundred and twenty-one miles. The Baltimore and Ohio is opened to Piedmont, twenty-eight miles west of Cumberland, and the rails are being laid over one hundred and sixty-five miles of new road. The George's Creek Railroad, from Cumberland to mines and iron works at Lonaconning, is also completed. Winans' new engines of the "Camel" type for the Baltimore and Ohio have nineteen-inch cylinders, with twenty-two-inch stroke, and three-feet-seven-inch wheels, the extreme wheel base being eleven feet three inches. The wheels are cast iron and have chilled rims, only the front and back pair having flanges. The foot plate for the two firemen is formed upon the tender, the engine-driver riding on top of the boiler. The weight of these engines is twenty-four and one-quarter tons, averaging six tons on each pair of wheels. Another type of engine introduced on the Baltimore and Ohio Railroad is known as the "Dutch Wagon." It has four driving wheels, and is used exclusively for passenger service. Thomas Winans named the "Celeste" after his wife, and this locomotive has eight wheels, four of them driving wheels without tires, being of chilled cast iron and in a single piece. The hubs are split, and fitted with keys and bands. The cab is forward, the reversing mechanism being worked from the front, and transmitted to the rear of the engine through tubes in the boiler. Ross Winans has patented a device for adding a cylinder over each of the great driving wheels of the engine "Carroll of Carrollton," so as to increase adhesion, which it does to a marked extent. Dr. Page, of Baltimore, who has for some time been experimenting with an electric motor, has finished the construction of a full-sized experimental machine, and it is the first to be propelled by electricity upon a railroad in the world. It is mounted upon four car wheels obtained from the railroad company, and the electric current as it has been applied propels the vehicle with more or less success. Several runs have been made with it on the Baltimore and Ohio, but the doctor encounters so much skepticism that he is not encouraged, and as a matter of fact cannot secure the necessary funds to carry his work beyond merely the experimental stage. Eddy, in a new type of locomotives, introduces for the first time the frame

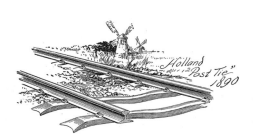

Midland Ry of India Nr 1890

Holland "12 Post Tie" 1890

Great Northern of Scotland 1890

with a splice ahead of the forward pedestal jaw to facilitate repairs. The "Gilmore" has drivers six feet nine inches in diameter, and horizontal cylinders fifteen and three-eighths inches by twenty-six inches. The engine is without a dome, and has a straight boiler with escape pipes. Mr. Eddy's original plan was to build the "Gilmore" with a single pair of driving wheels, but this he changed, and she is an eight-wheeler. An engine built at the Springfield shops of the Western Railroad of Massachusetts has fifteen and three-eighths inch horizontal cylinders, twenty-six-inch stroke, and a single pair of six-feet-nine-inch driving wheels. There are eleven and one-eighth square feet of grate surface, sixty-eight square feet of firebox heating surface, and one hundred and ninety-six tubes twelve feet four inches long and one and three-quarters inches in diameter, presenting one thousand one hundred and four square feet of heating surface. She has a single three and one-quarter inch blast pipe. Griggs, of the Boston and Providence Railroad, has completed two tank engines with cylinders nine inches in diameter, a sixteen-inch stroke, four and one-half foot wheels, and weighing eleven tons six hundred-weight each. The draw-bar is connected to levers which bear against the boxes of the driving wheels in order to increase the adhesive weight upon the driving wheels when at work, and the adhesion is thus increased in ratio following the increased resistance to be overcome. In a public contest between ten locomotives at Lowell one of these engines drew two long eight-wheel passenger coaches containing eighty-one passengers at a mean speed of forty-two miles an hour, the maximum speed maintained for three consecutive miles being at the rate of forty-eight miles an hour. The "Champlain" is an inside cylinder engine on the New York Central Railroad which is calling forth much favorable comment. The "Great Western Express," as the new locomotive on the Great Western Railway of England is named, has inside cylinders eighteen inches in diameter with a twenty-four-inch-stroke, eight-foot driving wheels, twenty-four square feet of grate surface, the barrel of the boiler being four feet six inches in diameter, and the cranks on the axle so far apart that the bottom of the boiler is brought down to a distance of only four feet eight inches above the rails and, of course, without interfering with them. The Hawthorns have obtained an English patent for compensating levers between the wheels of locomotive engines, fol-

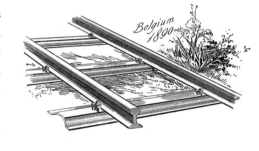

137

lowing very closely Harrison's practice in America. The "Hawthorn," the latest locomotive constructed by them, is of the six-wheeled inside-cylinder class and, it is claimed, will run safely at a speed of eighty miles an hour.

Albert Fink, who is the principal office assistant of Benjamin H. Latrobe, Chief Engineer of the Baltimore and Ohio Railroad, is practically the designer of the great iron bridge across the Monongahela River below the mouth of Tygart's Valley River, and which is one of the largest in the world. Wendell Bollman, the "Master of Road" of the company, has completed the first iron suspension bridges of noteworthy dimensions upon the line. Two of these are upon the Washington branch, and three upon the main line, one of the latter, that at Harper's Ferry, being one hundred and twenty-four feet in length. West of Piedmont there are thirty miles of gradients of one in forty-five and one-half, or one hundred and sixteen feet per mile, and others of one in fifty, with frequent curves of six hundred feet radius.

Winans' "Camel" engines of 1852, built for the Baltimore and Ohio, weigh in working order twenty-four tons, have wheels forty-three inches in diameter, cylinders nineteen inches in diameter with a stroke of twenty-two inches, boilers forty-six inches in diameter, with one hundred and three tubes of two and one-half inches outside diameter, and fourteen feet in length, and a grate seven feet long and three and one-half feet wide. Hayes, the Master of Machinery of the company, has added another pair of wheels to five engines of the "Camel" type he has built at the Mount Clare shops. These engines are therefore ten-wheelers, and they have cylinders twenty inches in diameter with a twenty-two-inch stroke, eight coupled wheels three feet seven inches in diameter, and weigh twenty-five and one-half tons. They have eighteen square feet of grate surface, and eighty-seven and one-half square feet of fire-box heating surface. Ross Winans in the "Centipede," his newest type of engine, reaches the enormous weight of forty-five tons, and she is the most powerful engine in existence. Her cylinders are twenty-two inches in diameter, with a twenty-two-inch stroke. There are eight coupled wheels three feet seven inches in diameter, and a swiveling truck in front, making twelve wheels in all, the truck being the first used with an independent side motion. The cross-heads and piston-rod are forged together. The cab is at the front end of the locomotive, and occupied only

138

by the engineer, the fireman's place being at the other end.   On a temporary line built over one of the tunnels that is in progress, Winans successfully works a nineteen-inch eight-coupled locomotive, which regularly ascends an incline slightly steeper than one in ten, or five hundred and thirty feet to the mile, drawing behind it the tender and an eight-wheeled loaded car weighing thirteen tons.   The weight of the engine is twenty-four and one-half tons, and when the coupled wheels are upon the incline of one in ten only nine-tenths of this weight, or say twenty-one and three-quarter tons, press effectively upon the rails.   The tender weighs twelve and three-quarter tons, and thus the aggregate of the whole train reaches fifty tons.   Seth Wilmarth has built for the Cumberland Valley Railroad two engines with cylinders twelve and one-half inches in diameter, a sixteen-inch stroke, and four cast-iron wheels with chilled rims three and one-half feet in diameter, located sixteen feet six inches from center to center.   Passenger engines with cylinders sixteen and one-half inches in diameter, a twenty-two-inch stroke, and four coupled wheels seven feet in diameter are the class most favored on the Hudson River Railroad. The sensational locomotive of the year is Milholland's "Illinois" on the Reading Road, it being the initial passenger engine on that line to burn anthracite coal, and the first really successful consumer of such fuel running into Philadelphia. This engine has two pair of seven-foot driving wheels, and has attained a speed of seventy-five miles an hour.   She was built in the Reading shops, and has cylinders seventeen inches in diameter, with a stroke of thirty inches.   The slide valve is double, with one plate at either end of the cylinder, while the link motion is operated by return cranks outside of the side rods.   Her weight is sixty-two thousand pounds.   Up to this time Chicago has not had a complete and uninterrupted line of railroad to the Eastern cities, but the Michigan Central is now open, and by connecting with the Lake Shore lines and the New York and Erie, there is a through all-rail route from the Atlantic to Lake Michigan.   The entire line of the Central Railroad of New Jersey, which is made up of a number of smaller corporations, has been completed and opened under a single management.   The Pennsylvania Railroad from Philadelphia to Pittsburg is virtually finished, although it has not as yet been formally established as a through route.

Zerah Colburn, in a number of six-ton tank engines designed by him for the three-feet-three-inch gauge in Canada, spreads the fire-box to a width greater than that of the gauge of the line by placing it entirely behind the wheels.   In

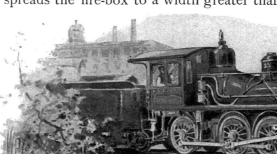

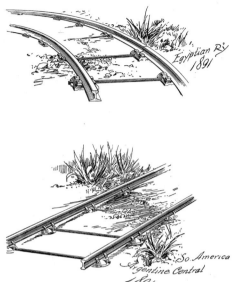

Egyptian R'y
1891

So. America
Argentine Central
1891

Germany the favorite type of locomotive is that used upon the railroads generally in the State of New Jersey. It has driving wheels behind the fire-box and two pair of forward wheels in a pivoted truck, permitting the passage of the engine around curves of small radius, an advantage of not such great importance in England as in Germany and America. McConnell, in England, in his latest engine has cylinders eighteen by twenty-four inches, and driving wheels seven feet six inches in diameter, all the six coupled wheels being under the barrel of the boiler. The locomotive "Bavaria," built by Maffei, of Munich, takes the principal prize of a series offered by the Austrian Government for engines each of which should draw a gross load of one hundred and ten tons in addition to its own weight and that of the tender, at the rate of ten miles an hour up a grade thirteen and one-quarter miles long on the north side of the Semmering, the average rise being one in forty-seven and the maximum for two and one-half miles one in forty. In the "Bavaria" the wheels of the tender are coupled to those of the engine by means of an endless chain, which, although it gives greater adhesion, is in operation attended by many difficulties. Engerth, the locomotive engineer of the Austrian Government, has constructed an engine and tender in such a manner that the side frames of the latter extend forward and past the fire-box, a portion of which they are made to support, and he is thus enabled to place one axle of the tender in front of the fire-box. The point at which the engine exerts its draft upon the tender is only a short distance behind the driving axle, and according to the curves of the lines the tender can move radially around this point. The peculiarity of the engine is that while the tender and locomotive are one, there is an elastic form of construction which permits the running of sharp curves, or of otherwise being operated as if separate. The front axle of the tender and the axle of the rear drivers each carry two toothed wheels, which engage intermediate wheels connected with the engine in such fashion that the entire ten wheels are controlled and move together notwithstanding the fact that the engines can move independently. The London and North Western Railroad Company has in use the largest inside-cylinder engines that it is believed can be operated upon the standard gauge. They are on six wheels and in working order weigh thirty-four and three-quarter tons. The cylinders are eighteen inches in diameter, the pistons having a stroke of twenty-four inches, and the driving wheels are seven feet in diameter. The six Stephenson

Mallet Compound 1891

140

engines for the Midland Railway have double frames, inside cylinders sixteen by twenty-two inches, and driving wheels six feet six inches in diameter. The railroad from St. Petersburg to Moscow in Russia is completed and opened for business. A man by the name of Waterbury has a patent for a closed space between the cars of a passenger train, the arrangement being such as to enable passengers to go in and out of the cars and from one to another with equal facility as in the usual construction. Atwood, a Connecticut mechanic, puts the Waterbury plan into execution on a train of the Naugatuck Railroad in Massachusetts, which is fitted up throughout to almost entirely do away with the dust and dirt formerly entering the cars at the ends, and which created so much discomfort. Trains on the Housatonic road and also on the lines of the New Jersey Railroad and Transportation Company are also being fitted up after the Atwood idea.

1853   The year 1853 marks the completion of the Baltimore and Ohio Railroad from Baltimore to Wheeling, three hundred and seventy-nine miles, and it is at this time the longest railroad in the world. Its construction has cost in round figures fifteen and a half millions of dollars, and the prediction of President Swan, made two years ago, that he would stand with his guests of the city of Baltimore and the States of Virginia and Maryland on the bank of the Ohio at Wheeling on January 1, 1853, has been fulfilled to the letter, the first through train reaching Wheeling on the day stated. The Central Ohio Railroad, from Wheeling through Zanesville to Newark and Columbus, and thence through Xenia to Cincinnati, is partly finished and in operation, and the remainder is under construction. The Parkersburg branch of the Baltimore and Ohio is also rapidly progressing. The English engine, "Brookline," built at the Bury Works, Liverpool, and imported by the Boston and Worcester Railroad in the thirties, originally had small wheels forward, after the English fashion, but she has been remodeled by the introduction of truck wheels and an extra pair of wheels in the rear of the drivers. In the "Boardman" boiler, which is in considerable use, a large flue extends from the fire-box directly through the smoke-box, a plate-iron partition being fixed quite close to the flue at about two-thirds of its length from the fire-box. A series of vertical tubes descends from the bottom of this flue, which is flat, to an ash-pan below, but by the interposition of the partition just mentioned the heated currents go down through about two-thirds of the tubes, and rise

141

again through the remainder, escaping thence, after having given off most of their heat, into the smoke-box. An air-pipe, perforated at its discharging end, is placed in the main flue to promote combustion. The Norrises have used the "Phleger" boiler in quite a number of their locomotives, it being notable for its hanging bridge and water wall, and for its fire-grate formed of water tubes. A ten-wheel freight engine built by them has six coupled wheels four feet in diameter, cylinder seventeen by twenty-four inches, and a boiler twenty-four feet long over all. The fire-box and combustion chamber is eleven feet long, while the tubes, two hundred and thirty in number and two inches in diameter, are the same length. The barrel of the boiler, three feet ten and one-half inches in diameter, is filled with tubes, and a large steam chamber formed above it. The New York Central Railroad Company, by act of Legislature of the State of New York, is formally constituted, the consolidation embracing the Albany and Schenectady, the Schenectady and Troy, the Utica and Schenectady, the Syracuse and Utica, the Rochester and Syracuse, the Buffalo and Lockport, the Mohawk Valley, the Buffalo and Rochester, Lockport and Niagara Falls railroad companies. The Rock Island road has been commenced. The population of Chicago is now increased to sixty-six thousand. The Atlantic and St. Lawrence Railroad in Canada is finished, and the line from New Haven to Montreal has been opened. The Pittsburgh, Fort Wayne and Chicago, between Pittsburg and Crestline, a distance of one hundred and eighty-seven miles, is also opened for business. The typical Mason engine is on eight wheels, four of which are drivers, coupled, and four in the leading truck with wide-spread wheel centers. The boiler is multitubular, with a wagon-top and deep fire-box between the front and back axles. The cylinders are connected under the smoke-box by a separate saddle, being level, with the usual four-guide, cross-head and the connecting-rod attached to a crankpin in the outside of the wheel. The valves are operated by two eccentrics and the usual link motion through a rock shaft. Mason is noted for his artistic taste as well as fine mechanical ability, and his type of locomotive is the most symmetrical and graceful of all American manufacturers. An engine by McQueen has outside connected cylinders set at an angle over the truck, the V hook valve motion, and Matthews' smoke-stack. Pear-

Webb's "Greater Britain" 1891

son, the Locomotive Superintendent of the Bristol and Exeter Railroad in England, has designed, and the Rothwells constructed, a broad-gauge tank engine with cylinders sixteen and one-half inches in diameter and a twenty-four-inch stroke. It has a single pair of driving wheels nine feet in diameter, and two trucks each containing four wheels four feet in diameter. The driving wheels have no flanges. India-rubber springs are applied under the axle bearings, and the weight of the engine, which has a trailing bogie, and is carried on ten wheels, is forty-two tons. The official test of this engine shows it will run smoothly at a speed of eighty miles an hour. The Bristol and Exeter, as well as the North London and the Great North of Scotland, have recognized the necessity of adapting the unyielding rectangular wheel base of heavy engines to sharper curves, and have adopted the "bogie" truck, and this device has also been applied by English and Scotch makers to engines for railways in Nova Scotia, Chili, and India.

Zerah Colburn is building, at the New Jersey Locomotive Works in Paterson, an engine with cylinders eighteen by twenty-four inches and six coupled wheels four feet in diameter. The fire-box is placed entirely between the driving wheels, and thus a width of seven feet six inches is obtained for the grate, the box being six feet long, and having an area of forty-five square feet. It is being constructed for a six-foot gauge and to burn anthracite coal. Baldwin has built for the Virginia Central Railroad, from designs by Charles Ellett, a class of tank locomotives especially designed for the heavy gradients and sharp curves over one of the tunnels now in course of construction through the Blue Ridge. The line has an average rise of one in twenty and one-half on the eastern, and one in twenty-three and two-thirds on the western slope, and to enable the engines to better adapt themselves to the road, the front and middle pair of drivers are held in position by wrought-iron beams having cylindrical boxes in each for the journal bearings, which beams vibrate on a pin fixed in the frame of the engine on each side, and resting upon the centers of the beams. The engines have outside cylinders sixteen and one-half inches in diameter with a twenty-inch stroke, six coupled wheels three and one-half feet in diameter, with a wheel base of nine feet four inches, their weight in working order being twenty-   four and one-half tons. The "Calhoun" is an engine with   two boilers, each forty-three inches in diameter, each having its own levelling steam space,

the steam from the lower boiler being conveyed through a large pipe into the dome above. She has cylinders nineteen inches in diameter with a thirty-inch stroke, ten-foot driving-wheels, and weighs thirty-six tons. A German-American type of locomotive of the Eastwick and Harrison class, has forward wheels embodied in a swiveling truck, with four coupled driving wheels at either end of the fire-box. In a plan followed in another engine, the driving wheels are placed together back of the fire-box. The main rod being connected to the front wheels is found to frequently cause heated journals, which has been obviated by injecting a stream of water from the tender. The fire-box is inside the boiler. John Cochran exhibits at the Fair of the Mechanics' Institute, in Baltimore, a model of a four-cylinder engine. The entire line of the Pennsylvania Railroad from Harrisburg to Pittsburgh is completed and opened for business, the construction being such as to avoid all inclined planes in crossing the Alleghenies.

France in 1855 furnishes the most striking example of the development of 1855 the large driving wheel on the four foot eight and a half inch gauge, in the locomotive "L'Aigle," designed by Blavier and Larpent, and constructed by Gouin, of Paris, for the Western Railway. The engine has four coupled driving wheels nine feet four inches in diameter, her cylinders being sixteen and a half inches in diameter, with a thirty-one and one-half inch stroke. The "L'Aigle" is in the Paris Exposition of this year, and attracts great attention. Gooch has a new type of engine upon the Great Western Railway in England, which has been constructed from his designs by Stephenson, it having two pairs of seven-foot driving wheels coupled, instead of one pair of eight-foot wheels, which has been the practice. There are now in operation in Great Britain eight thousand two hundred and ninety-seven miles of railroad, costing $1,487,420,000.

Milholland, following up his experience with the "Illinois," his initial anthracite-burning passenger locomotive, has completed for the Philadelphia and Reading Railroad the first of his double-flue section engines. The two sections are divided by a combustion chamber, which is between them and just over the center pair of drivers, and the cylinders are eighteen by twenty-two inches. Rogers, of Paterson, gives the preference to outside-cylinder engines, and is among the first to counterbalance the reciprocating as well as the revolving parts, and place the cylinders in a nearly horizontal position, lengthening the truck-wheel base in order to obtain room for them. He strengthens the fastenings of the cylinders, and otherwise makes the present type

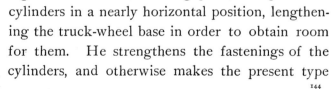

Roger's Compound 1891

superior to the inside-cylinder engine. The Parkersburg branch of the Baltimore and Ohio is finished, and the entire line from the Chesapeake Bay to Cincinnati is now in operation. The completion of the Sunbury and Erie Railroad enables direct connection with Baltimore and Philadelphia. The Lehigh Valley Railroad is finished from Easton to Allentown. The great suspension bridge at Niagara Falls is open for the passage of trains. The Chicago, Burlington and Quincy is in operation for one hundred and forty miles, or from Galesburg to a junction of the Galena Road, thirty miles west of Chicago. The Dixon Air Line and the Chicago and Rock Island Railroads are also in full operation. The engine " Pioneer," built by the Manchester Locomotive Works, has outside-connected horizontal cylinders, spread truck, and wagon-top boiler. The Rogers' " Madison " has spread truck with outside bearings, outside-connected cylinders, which are slightly inclined, wagon-top boiler, and two domes.

1856   The Engerth type of engine with certain modifications is adopted in 1856 for a number of very large freight engines for the Eastern Railway of France. Some forty engines have been built on the Engerth system by various makers, among them Schneider, of Creusote. The coupling of the tender to the engine at a point in front of the fire-box by extending the frame of the former some distance in front of the latter is the special feature of the Engerth engines, but this same end was accomplished twenty or more years ago by Ross Winans in his engines by using a draft or pulling bar upwards of ten feet in length and three and one-half inches in diameter, which passed through the ash-pan and coupled the engine and tender together in front of the fire-box. Engerth's engines on the French line weigh in working order nearly forty-one tons. The tender, which really forms a component part of the engine, weighs when loaded twenty-one tons more, making the total weight sixty-two tons. The Neilsons, of Glasgow, Scotland, have produced a single-cylinder locomotive of simple design for mineral traffic. It has four coupled wheels, the cylinder is horizontal and placed under the fire-box end of the boiler, the piston-rod works through the back head, and a long cross-head spanning the width of the engine gives motion to a pair of connecting-rods, which work upon pins in the driving wheels. The connecting-rods are made to work at right angles to each other, in order to avoid dead points and to prevent any chance of the connecting-rods taking opposite directions at the commencement of the stroke. Jouffray and Sequier, of France, have labored for years to increase adhesion,

Paris & Orleans
1892

and develop power through adding weight to locomotives in such a manner as not to be attended by the difficulties met with in the ordinary engine of the period. Jouffray's plan is a good deal after the idea of the "Coffee Roaster" coal cars, as they were called when introduced on the Baltimore and Ohio years ago. These were enormous drums or cylindrical-shaped con- trivances, planned so the outer edge would fit the rails. Through the doors or other openings provided they were completely filled with coal, and then rolled along like huge hogsheads in the trail of the horses or engines which were used to pull them. Jouffray places his engine upon one carriage and his boiler upon another, with a single pair of wheels for each. These are simply the carrying wheels, as the power is communicated to a very large wheel in front, which runs upon a center rail. Baldwin's "Tiger" has outside connected inclined cylinders and a straight boiler with two domes. A Murray and Hazlehurst engine of the "Dutch Wagon" type for the Baltimore and Ohio has inside-connected cy- linders, a wagon-top boiler, and one dome forward. The record of the construc- tion of railroads in the United States to this time reaches three thousand four hundred and eight miles, making a total in operation of twenty-three thousand three hundred and forty-two miles. In France there are four thousand and thirty-eight miles in operation, costing equal to $616,000,000.

Early in 1857 Bissell patents a most important improvement in the truck. 1857 In its original form only the truck axles could take a practically radial position on a curve, and the driving and trailing wheels assumed nearly the same position on a curve which they would have if an ordinary single leading axle occupied the place of the pivot of the truck. In the "Bissell" truck the load is taken upon the center as in the swiveling trucks in common use in American engines, but the angular motion, instead of taking place around a pivot between the truck axles, is defined by a radial framing working around a stud or king-bolt at some distance behind the truck, and not far from the driving axle.

Milholland's great twelve-wheel locomotive, the "Pennsylvania," is at work on the Reading road, and contrary to the arguments advanced prior to its completion, is found well adapted for use upon curves even sharper than twenty degrees. The "Pennsyl- vania" has outside horizontal cylinders twenty inches in diameter with a twenty-six-inch stroke of piston, and twelve coupled wheels three feet seven inches in diameter, each pair being three feet eleven

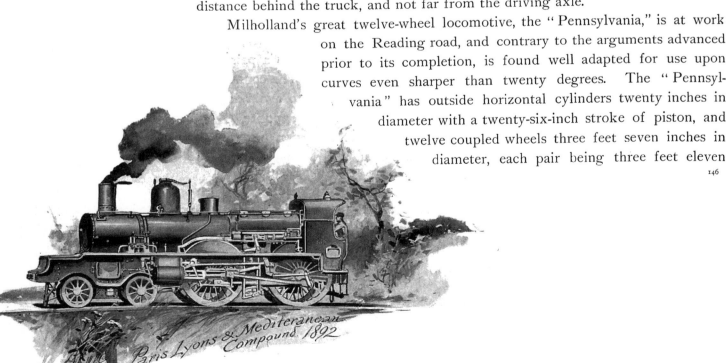

Paris Lyons & Mediterraneau Compound 1892

inches between centers, giving a wheel base of nineteen feet seven inches. The grate, formed of water tubes, through which a constant circulation is maintained, is nine feet long and three and one-half feet wide, presenting thirty-one and one-half square feet of surface. The boiler is four feet in diameter, and excluding a combustion chamber two feet one inch long, contains one hundred and seventy-four iron tubes two inches in diameter and thirteen feet six inches long, and has a total heating surface of one thousand three hundred and twenty-eight square feet. The three water tanks contain one thousand two hundred and twenty-four gallons. No coal is carried except upon the grate, the fire being replenished at either end of the line, the special purpose of the locomotive being the assisting of heavy coal trains upon a gradient one and one-half miles long having an inclination of one in one hundred and fifty-five. The extreme length of the engine is thirty-six feet, and its weight in working order fifty tons. The Ohio and Mississippi is open to Vincennes, and the Mississippi and Missouri Railroad extended from Davenport to Iowa City. The Illinois Central is completed and in operation its entire length, but being overwhelmed by a floating debt of several millions of dollars, is compelled to make an assignment. The Pennsylvania Railroad has secured control of the Pennsylvania canals. On the Erie road it is decided to replace iron with steel rails whenever renewals are made. The twenty-seven thousand miles which are now in operation in the United States cost $920,000,000. British roads cost an average of $179,000 per mile, French roads an average of $152,000 per mile, and American roads an average of $35,000 per mile. Cudworth, of the Southeastern Railway in England, is adopting for the locomotives of that road the long inclined double grate, with alternate firing through each door, and with the opportunity for mixing and ignition of the gas and air in front of the longitudinal midfeather, this being found to be an effective form of fire-box.

1858   Baldwin, in 1858, for the first time places his cylinders horizontally. The Pennsylvania Railroad is open from Allentown to Reading, establishing a direct line with unbroken gauge to Harrisburg, Pittsburgh, and the West. Ramsbottom has at the Crewe Works, for the Manchester and Birmingham Railroad, a new "goods" or freight engine with inside frames and inside bearings only, inside cylin-

147

ders seventeen by twenty-four inches, and six coupled wheels five feet in diameter. In 1859 he places the "Problem," his first express engine, upon the 1859 Northern Division, with cylinders sixteen by twenty-four inches. Sixteen-wheel passenger coaches are introduced upon several American lines. These coaches are supported at the extremities by a swiveling frame, each end of which is in its turn borne by an ordinary four-wheel truck. A passenger carriage of this character has been made at Springfield and exported to Egypt for the private use of the Viceroy. The Chicago and Northwestern Railroad is open for business from Chicago to Oshkosh, one hundred and ninety-four miles. The Mississippi is reached by the Memphis and Charleston road. Giffards' injector or boiler-feeder is applied to the English locomotive by Ramsbottom, his "Problem" being the first upon which it is used. It promises to in a great extent supplant the force pumps generally employed. Giffards' discovery is, that the motion imparted by a jet of steam to a surrounding column of water is sufficient to force it into a boiler working at an even higher pressure. Thus the water in the boiler will rush out of an opening at the bottom with the same velocity as that with which the water will escape from the bottom of a reservoir in which the head is such as to cause the same pressure per square inch. The "Princess Royal," on the London and Great Western road in England, is a six-wheel engine, with one pair leading, one pair driving, and one pair trailing. She has outside-connected cylinders placed on an incline over the leading wheels, and a central dome on a straight boiler. Berkley, on the inclines of the Great India and Peninsular Railway of India, adopts the system of working tank engines in pairs, employing one engineer and two firemen. The Thul Gat incline is nine and one-half miles long, and of this four miles are on a continuous gradient of one in thirty-seven. The tank engines designed for this work have cylinders fifteen inches in diameter with a twenty-two-inch stroke, and four coupled wheels four feet in diameter. Each engine weighs thirty-four and one-half tons, of which nearly sixteen tons are on one axle and eighteen tons on the other.

The Ramsbottom self-feeding tender of 1860 replenishes the water in the 1860 tender while the train is in rapid motion. It is accomplished by troughs of cast iron four hundred and forty-one yards long, with a further length at each end of sixteen yards, rising one in one

St Petersburgh & Warsaw
1892

148

hundred. They are eighteen inches wide and seventeen inches deep, and placed between the rails, so that water five inches deep stands about the level of the rails. The tender of the ordinary pattern, holding fifteen hundred gallons, is provided with a rising water pipe, the lower end of which is fitted with an adjustable scoop ten inches wide at the mouth. Beugmot's locomotives on the Paris, Lyons and Mediterranean Railway in France are designed for greater tractive force and flexibility of motion than is possessed by the Engerth engines. The " La Rampe " and the " La Courbe," built by Koechlin, of Mulhouse, are upon Beugmont's plans, the cylinders being twenty-one and one-quarter inches in diameter, with a stroke of twenty-two inches. They are placed five feet one and one-quarter inches from center to center, and directly in front of the leading wheels, which are the drivers of the engines. The piston rods extend through the front cylinder heads, and by means of stout cross-heads, work the driving wheels through a pair of connecting rods turning respectively an outside crank and a crank in the driving axle. The axles of the four pairs of coupled wheels are provided with both outside and inside axle boxes.

THE Evolution and Development of the Rail Way of the World have been followed in more or less detail to the year 1860. As it would be impossible to continue what may be termed the period of modern progress, with a corresponding fulness, within the confines of a single volume, it has been deferred to a later work, in the preparation of which unexampled opportunities will be afforded for data and personal information.

Of direct interest in connection with the Evolution and Development of the Rail Way of the World, as delineated in the foregoing pages, must be the fact that full-size working reproductions and originals, something over fifty examples, illustrating the thought, the inception, and the evolution, are in existence.

When the Baltimore and Ohio Railroad Company determined upon making an exhibit at the World's Columbian Exposition in Chicago, the author of this work, who had been in the service of the Company for several years,

Johnstone
Double Bogie
Compound
1892

and thoroughly informed as to its history, was called into conference, which resulted in his being empowered to submit a plan for representation at Chicago commensurate with the part this single corporation had played in the origin, the
growth, and perfection of the railway.

Even with the year and a half allotted, it, at the first blush, appeared a task with
very many difficulties to surmount to encompass a graphic and comprehensive
showing of the evolution of the one railroad, the Baltimore and Ohio, the oldest
on the American continent, and in the true sense the oldest railway in the world,
it having been formally opened for public business six months prior to the Liverpool and Manchester in England. It is true the Stockton and Darlington had
been opened five years before, but it was not a rail, rather a tramway, built and
operated by a coal company for its and not the public's convenience. Incident-
ally it was used by the travelling public, but only as such employment did not
interfere with the actual purpose of construction—the transport of the product of
the mines to tide-water. As late as a year after the Liverpool and Manchester
had been opened, or in the early "thirties," there were a half dozen or more outside contractors running coaches over the Stockton and Darlington, subject to
restrictions which hardly brought the line within the category some historians have
essayed to place it. As a rule the Liverpool and Manchester is regarded by the
acknowledged authorities as the pioneer railway, not only of England but of
Europe, and indeed it was quite generally referred to, during the period of its
construction, as "the great British experimental railway." However, it is not the
present purpose to enter into argument relative to one or another historical fact.
It is very often the case that at such distance from the actual occurrence, different
people see with different eyes, and not infrequently the wish is father to the
thought. It may be so in this instance, and recognizing that man is not infallible,
the question as to which was actually the first railway will be suffered to lie over
until a further and possibly more auspicious occasion. Suffice it now to affirm,
without fear of contradiction, that the Baltimore and Ohio was the first to recognize the importance of an adequate representation at an Exposition of the greatest single interest in the world—the railway.

As the matter of the representation at Chicago was dwelt upon
in all its possibilities, the conclusion was finally reached that to com-
prehensively illustrate the inception and growth upon a basis which
would afford an intelligent study, the proper procedure would be
the embracing of all important stages from the first thought,

150

Erie Decapod
1893

that of Sir Isaac Newton, in 1680, to the hundred-ton locomotive of modern times. This was a broad and liberal basis from which to view the situation, and it cannot be regarded as out of place to refer to the fact that the Baltimore and Ohio Company in what it actually accomplished gave less prominence to itself than to others when aggregating them in comparison with the number of its own examples shown. In other words, there was in reality more in the exhibit that did not directly pertain to the Baltimore and Ohio than did; but the importance and value of the whole was correspondingly greater in that selfishness did not govern. The exhibit was made with a realizing sense of the opportunity that reflected credit on the Company, and was in keeping with the breadth and spirit actuating the Exposition in almost, if not all, its departments.

The subject was one of the deepest interest, and at the same time of no ordinary concern, as there had never been an attempt made to illustrate the railway historically upon anything approaching a fitting scale. The connection between the past and present was mostly comprised in publications only more or less complete, while the relics, original records, drawings, prints, and the like, still preserved, were widely scattered.

A course of study was entered upon by the writer, which subsequently led him to visit Europe, and the co-operation at once extended him on part of the institutions where historical locomotives and other examples of early railroading are treasured, was such as to constitute a large incentive to reach results even beyond those originally contemplated.

Commencing with the thought of Isaac Newton, which is the first looking to the propulsion by steam on land that history records, the idea was put in form, and the reproduction of the theory of 1680 was as if it had been actually constructed of a size for use.

Next came the "Cugnot" of 1769, built from the drawings and photographs furnished by the authorities of the Conservatoire des Arts et Métiers in Paris, where the original is preserved. This was followed by the "Murdoch" of 1780, constructed from the drawings and photographs se- cured of the model in the possession of one of the descendants of the inventor. The "Read" of 1791, the first idea of propulsion by steam on land on the American continent, the full-size working reproduction made from the drawings and specifications by Read himself, and filed in the Patent Office. These were of the very few saved from the

Brook's Tandem Compound
1895

fire which in the "forties" destroyed so many of the records of the United States Patent Office.

Then the "Trevithick" of 1800, which, at the best, was never more than an experimental model, and which, in order to preserve the continuity of the reproductions, that they might be studied in connection with the originals in the exhibit, was built full size, that is to say, of such dimensions as it might have been had the inventor determined to attempt actual results in his maiden effort. He, however, did not, and as a matter of fact the model from which the more or less speculative reproduction was constructed was on a scale so small as to enable its being operated on a kitchen-table. Immediately following this representation was a full-size reproduction of the real locomotive built by Trevithick, 1803–4, the first to move on rails in the world.

Speaking of them in chronological order, the manner in which they were placed in the exhibit, next came the "Evans" of 1804, the initial propulsion by steam on land on the American continent, and the first practical movement by head of steam in the world, inasmuch as the "Evans," weighing some twenty tons, was actually propelled through the streets of Philadelphia by its own power, and up to this time nothing of similar weight had before been moved by steam either upon rail or common road. The "Trevithick" of 1808, the first seen in London, and practically the last effort of the Father of the locomotive in this line, as, at the best, he made but a very scanty living, and found he could insure scarcely this in other directions.

The "Brunton," 1812, the "horse leg" as it was called, two or three of the type having been built with the idea that there should be some purchase on the track or road-bed in order to insure adhesion. Hedley's model of 1813, through which he was the first to demonstrate in a practical way the adhesion of smooth wheels to smooth rails. Hedley's "Puffing Billy" was constructed immediately after the successful experiment with the model. This locomotive, the oldest in the world, is preserved in the South Kensington Museum in London, and the full-size working reproduction constructed was from the detail drawings and plans made from the measurements of the actual engine, furnished by the authorities of the Museum. The "Blenkinsop" of 1813, built and run by cog gearing, working into the track on one side. The "Blucher," 1816, George Stephenson's first locomotive. The "Seguin," 1826–27, the first locomotive in the world with multitubular boiler. The "Howard," 1828, the first locomotive patented in America, and built from

152

Brooks
1893

the original drawings and specifications filed in the United States Patent Office. George Stephenson's "Rocket," the winner of the prize at the Liverpool and Manchester competition of 1829, constructed from the tracings of the original drawings furnished by the Stephenson Company. Hackworth's "Sans Pareil," which engine is also preserved in the South Kensington Museum, the original having been measured, and detail drawings furnished of it by the Director of that institution. Ericsson's "Novelty" of 1820, the first tank locomotive, and the creation of the afterward so distinguished an inventor. The "Stourbridge Lion" of the same year, the first locomotive ever operated upon American soil, it having been built on a then approved English type by Foster and Raistrick. The "Cooper" of 1830, the first locomotive built in America. The original "York," "Child," "Costell," and the "James," the four engines taking part in the Baltimore and Ohio competition, the successful one of which was the "York." This engine was almost immediately thereafter remodelled by Ross Winans, and a full-size working reproduction was included in the exhibit in its original form, and another in its approved shape, the latter constituting the father of the American type of the so-called "grasshopper" engine. The "Mercury," 1830, George Stephenson's highest development, and the first of the "Planet" type. The "Best Friend," the first locomotive built on the American continent for actual use. The "Old Ironsides," Baldwin's first locomotive. The "James" of 1832, the first locomotive in the world with the link motion. Horatio Allen's "South Carolina," the first eight-wheel locomotive in the world, as also the first double-ender. Jervis' "Experiment" of the same year, the first locomotive in the world constructed with the forward or "bogie" truck. The "Atlantic," the original "grasshopper" engine of 1832, and the oldest locomotive in America. The "Traveller," of 1833, also an original engine built by Davis, and the first of a distinctive type for freight purposes. The "Mazeppa" of 1836, originally a "grasshopper," but the cylinders subsequently altered from the vertical to the horizontal, constituting the first of the "Crab" type. The "Jefferson" of 1836, a fourth original engine, and illustrating the highest form of the "grasshopper" development of that year. The "Campbell," 1836, a full-size working reproduction made from the original drawings in the possession of the Baldwin Locomotive Works, and the father of the standard type of eight-wheel American engines. The "Hercules" of 1837, the first in the world with equalizing beams and levers. The "La Fayette" 1837, il-

153

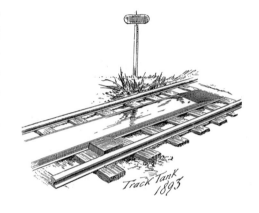

Track Tank
1893

"Number 999"
N.Y.C.R.R.
1893

lustrating the Norris development at that time, and similar in construction to the "Philadelphia," the locomotive which created so great a sensation in England, where it successfully surmounted the Lickey Incline, and led to the doing away with chain power, which up to that time had been used in the operation of the incline.

The "Sandusky," 1837, the first of the Rogers engines, and the first locomotive west of the Ohio River. The "Rocket," 1838, of the Philadelphia and Reading Railroad, the original engine by Braithwaite, of England, and the first on the line named. The original locomotive "Samson," built by Hackworth, in 1839, and the first in Nova Scotia, and with the original passenger coach it drew. The "Albion," 1839, also an original engine, and the second sent to Nova Scotia by Hackworth. Winans' "Buffalo," 1842, the first eight-wheel coupled locomotive in the world, and the first of the "Mud Digger" type. The "Mount Clare," 1844, the first locomotive built by the Baltimore and Ohio Company in its own shops. Winans' "Camel," 1846, the first of the type, and the pioneer of the large, heavy-draught locomotives. The "Dragon," 1848, the original engine, and Baldwin's first use of the rocking-grate. The ten-wheel "Camel," 1850, also an original engine. The "Mason," 1856, another original engine, and the only one of the famous type in its original form in existence. The original engine "Peppersauce," 1862, the first mountain-climbing locomotive in the world. The "Perkins," 1864, likewise an original engine, and first of the powerful locomotives with capacity to draw heavy trains over the grades of the Allegany mountains. The "600," the first passenger mogul engine, and exhibited by the Baltimore and Ohio Railroad, at whose shops it was built, at the Centennial, at Philadelphia, in 1876. The modern examples, illustrating the development of the Columbian Exposition year, were a standard eight-wheel passenger locomotive, and a standard ten-wheel freight engine, together with the "Director General," a Baldwin compound eight-wheel passenger locomotive, weighing in working order approximately one hundred tons.

The space filled by this representation of evolution and development was something over thirty-six thousand square feet, the greatest area occupied by a single exhibit in the entire Exposition. In addition to the examples enumerated, there were numerous collections of the highest historical value, examples of early tram-plates, rails, chair, and joints, dating back beyond the century. Plates, joints, and stones of the tramway on which the first

Pennsylvania R.R. 1893

locomotive ran in 1804, five of the original rails, with their chairs, on which the Liverpool and Manchester locomotive contest occurred in 1829; a section of the original track, with its granite sills and strap-iron rail, on which the Baltimore and Ohio competition took place a year or so later. There were also two of the original cars drawn by the "Trevithick" of 1804; and the implements used by Charles Carroll, the last surviving signer of the Declaration of Independence, in laying the corner-stone of the Baltimore and Ohio Railroad in 1828.

A prominent feature of the exhibit as a whole was the great gallery of original drawings, prints, photographs, and the like, numbering upwards of seventeen hundred, and illustrating in these various ways something of the railway history, progress, development, and operation in every country in the world wherein a locomotive whistle has been heard. The series of original drawings was undoubtedly the most valuable and important ever gathered together, the making of the collection involving an immense extent of detail. The correspondence in the general consummation of the plans embraced all countries and aggregated over seven thousand letters.

The greatest care was taken to insure accuracy in the representations both as to the reproductions and the perfection of the historical record. In many instances descendants of the pioneer inventors and operators were communicated with, through advertisements inserted in leading papers asking address, and numerous journeys were made to different sections in order to meet those in interest personally. There was a disinclination, at first at least, to permit many of the old drawings, prints, and documents to pass from the actual possession of those who had treasured them so long, but such confidence was finally established as to lead to their being loaned for the purpose of exhibition. It would not be practicable to attempt to mention the large number to whom there will ever be an indebtedness for the co-operation given. Nevertheless it is the strong desire to acknowledge it in an unequivocal manner, and it is hoped that this will be accepted as such by those without whose aid the results attained would not have been possible. It was truly without limit, extending as it did throughout the whole world. Often the highest confidence was manifested by those in the most remote lands, the acquaintance with whom was wholly through correspondence. Certainly no more agreeable or encouraging task was ever conducted by any one than that of the writer in the preparation of the great collection, the interest in which was everywhere manifested to a degree never

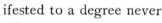

before experienced. It is not the purpose in this publication to attempt a review of the features which rendered the Department of Transportation Exhibits so striking an innovation in the history of World's Expositions. It is in much more competent hands, and as it should be without the necessity for curtailment to any prescribed limit. It is, however, eminently proper, as it is unqualifiedly due, that recognition should be specially recorded of the hearty co-operation and the earnest participation in the general plan followed in the preparation of the Baltimore and Ohio exhibit by the Chief of the Department, Mr. Willard A. Smith. From the very first inception of the scope of the collection, he entered into it with the warmest zeal, not permitting the scepticism of those who questioned its full accomplishment to militate in his granting of space, and the writer unhesitatingly acknowledges that to Mr. Smith is very much more to be credited than can be expressed in words.

Not only is this true as regards the work, the preparation, and the actual administration during the Exposition period; but following it, when the question arose as to the final disposition of the unparalleled collection, that is to say, the means to be adopted to insure its preservation for all time.

THE movement looking to the establishment of the Columbian Museum as a memorial of the Exposition had, at first, little or no tendency toward the mechanical. There was no hesitation in recognizing the great value of the railway exhibit, but there was a feeling that the immense space that would be required to preserve it presented difficulties necessitating no ordinary thought to overcome.

Long before the full completion of the collection the writer had become deeply impressed with the importance of profiting by the opportunity to establish the pioneer Museum of the World's Rail Way. The historical locomotives and other relics of the past belonging to the various institutions of the world, were, to a more or less extent, preserved as curiosities, and not in connection with any systematic showing which would enable study. There was no continuity in the relics as possessed, and this, as a matter of course, operated against their being so placed as to constitute series of object-lessons. The practice followed in the preparation of the Baltimore and Ohio collection, of supplying full-size working reproductions to fill the missing links in the chain of Evolution and Development, met the requirements in so insuring the showing as a whole that history could be followed link by link, and this, together with the contributions which came from all parts of the world, led to a completion which, the larger the comprehension of its value the greater the disinclination to leave any effort unattempted to bring about the preservation as a whole. In this feeling Mr. Smith shared, and the official decision on the part of the Columbian Museum authorities to provide for the railway exhibit, if it could be secured, was at once accepted as the initial move toward making the Museum of the World's Rail Way a certainty.

Meantime the Pennsylvania Railroad Company, which had, through Mr. Theo. N. Ely, Chief of Motive Power, and his immediate representative, Prof. J. Elfreth Watkins, perfected a remarkably complete and valuable exhibit, illustrative through the fullest detail, of the history of the greatest of railway corporations, most heartily seconded the movement looking to the formation of the Railway Museum, and announced the intention of placing the collection in it. After due deliberation the Baltimore and Ohio decided to present outright the entire exhibit illustrative of the Evolution and Development of the Rail Way of the World to the Museum, and this was done. The whole east wing of the Art Palace at Jackson Park, Chicago, the edifice which was preserved and made the temporary home of the Museum, was set aside for the Railway Museum, and before the summer had fully set in the work of remodelling it, which was inaugurated during the winter, was completed, and the collections installed under the personal direction and supervision of the writer.

Mr. Ayer, President of the Museum, having himself a large railroad experience, at once appreciated the value and importance of adding to the interest of the collection by showing each original or reproduction upon the track of its period. This rule was followed in the installation, and therefore the nucleus for a complete Museum of Permanent Way was secured, the original rail chairs, stones, ties, etc., being used as far as possessed, and reproductions perfected in other instances. The interest displayed by the various railway companies in the Museum was s p e e d i l y manifested through gift to it of such as would appropriately be included in its various divisions. The Illinois Central presented the

157

Pittsburg Compound 1893

original old locomotive of 1832–6, which was run on the Ponchartrain Railway near New Orleans, and the Chicago and Northwestern Railroad contributed the old locomotive " Pioneer," the first in Chicago. Numerous exhibitors interested in the railway and its appliances presented series of drawings and photographs, and in quite a number of instances examples of actual construction, some of them of the very highest historical value. While owing to the lack of room, and pending the perfection of plans which are under contemplation, the New York Central and Hudson River Railroad Company still retain the full-size reproduction of the first railway train in New York, headed by the " De Witt Clinton," the locomotive and coaches, as well as other portions of the exhibit made by the Company in Chicago, it is the announced purpose to present these to the Railway Museum in Chicago. A similar situation exists as regards two or three prominent English companies ; and when the opportunity will permit there is no question as to the Museum being carried forward to a point where its possessions will be equal to more than double those now within its walls.

It is not, however, the sole purpose of the Museum authorities to perpetuate the Railway Museum simply upon lines embracing historical features of progress, but to so perfect its organization as to render it something more than such, in fact, an institution of the railway worthy in every respect of the interest represented.

THE total mileage of the railways of the United States is a hundred and seventy-six thousand, and the capital invested ten and a half billions ; the gross earnings reaching a billion and a quarter of dollars. The earnings of the railway companies are thus equal to a sum almost, if not quite, three times the entire revenue of the United States Government. They are thirty per cent greater than the whole of the exports of the United States, while the investments in railroads equalled seven times the actual money in circulation in the United States, and over twelve times the net public debt of the United States at the close of the fiscal year, June 30, 1803. The railway earnings of the United States were in volume nearly a quarter of a billion of dollars greater than the value of the combined production of wheat, corn, and oats, three times the total value of the cotton produced, double the value of the production of lumber, four

158

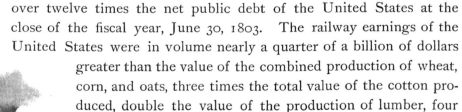

times the value of the metallic product—gold, silver, iron, copper, lead, etc., three times the value of the non-metallic product — coal, stone, etc., etc., and equaled the value of the output of the whole manufacturing industries of the country. All the coin gold in the United States produced in the century from 1792 to 1892 did not by considerable equal a sum double that of the railway earnings of 1893, while the coining value of the silver produced in the country did not by more than a hundred millions of dollars equal the railway earnings for the one year.

The annual earnings of the railways of the United Kingdom aggregate within but eight per cent. of the entire revenue of the government, and the capital invested in the railways is thirty-five per cent. greater than the whole debt of the Kingdom. One-half of the exports of the United States are to Great Britain, and large as is the aggregate, representative of something like four hundred millions, it is practically only a sum equal to the annual earnings of the British railways. The total output of mineral in the United Kingdom, metallic and non-metallic (including coal, which of itself yields three hundred and thirty millions of dollars) barely equals the summation of the railway earnings, while the aggregated worth of the textile products, in which England leads the world, is but ten per cent. greater than the railway revenue.

Russia has a railway mileage of twenty-three thousand, in which the equivalent of three and three-quarter billions of dollars have been invested, and from which there is two hundred and seventy millions revenue. Railway construction has been pushed forward throughout the empire with extraordinary vigor, this being strikingly the fact as regard the Trans-Siberian and Trans-Caspian systems. The former has been determined upon to the extreme limits of the Czar's domain on the Sea of Japan—Vladivostock—and subsequently when the system is extended to the Pacific at Behring Straits there will scarcely be more than forty miles of water intervening between its terminus and the Alaskan possessions of the United States. This great line to the Japan Sea, which will embrace five thousand miles of track, is being constructed upon an estimated expenditure of one hundred and twenty millions of dollars, and its completion is promised by 1905. One day it will in part be of the Asiatic and European divisions of the greatest trunk line of railway the world can ever know, one that with its American connections and its European divisions, will make it possible to pass by rail around the larger portion of the globe, from, in fact, New York on the western shore of the Atlantic, to Lisbon, exactly opposite on the eastern side, with less than a forty-

Royal Blue
Day Coach
1893

B&O Standard 1893

mile width of water to encompass on the entire journey of approximating twelve thousand miles.

Germany has a railway mileage of twenty-seven thousand, in which have been invested upward of two and a half billions of dollars. As comparisons have been made between the earnings of the railways of Great Britain and the governmental revenues of the Kingdom, a like contemplation in Germany is interesting, as it shows that the gross earnings of the railways are twenty-three and a half million dollars greater than the entire governmental revenues of the empire.

Of the capital invested in the world's railways, equal to nearly thirty-three billions of dollars, the United States has ten and a half billions, or more than one-third; England and Wales nearly four billions, or not quite one-eighth; Russia three and a quarter billions, or upward of one-tenth; Germany over two and a half billions, say one-fifteenth, and France over two and a quarter billions, or nearly a fifteenth.

Of the gross earnings, equaling three and a quarter billions of dollars, the United States has a billion and a quarter, or more than one-third; England three hundred and fifty millions, or nearly one-ninth; Germany three hundred and thirty-eight millions, or something over one-tenth; Russia two hundred and seventy millions, or one-eleventh; and France two hundred and thirty-two millions, or one-thirteenth.

Of the mileage, aggregating over four hundred thousand, the United States has one hundred and seventy odd thousand, or nearly seven-fifteenths; Germany twenty-seven thousand, or a little over one-fifteenth; Russia twenty-three thousand, or not quite one-fifteenth; India twenty thousand, or one twenty-first; Austria-Hungary and France over eighteen thousand, or a trifle less than one twenty-second each; Canada and Belgium both over fourteen thousand, or each one twenty-eighth.

WHEN it was determined to found the pioneer Museum of the World's Rail Way as a component part of the Field Columbian Museum, there was an accompaying decision to constitute a commission which should visit every country in the world where the railway had penetrated. This that there might be knowledge of the actual development gained through personal investigation, that communication should be established between

Rogers 1893

the various countries and the Museum, contributions secured, interest stimulated by explanation of the purposes of the institution, and a system of correspondence perfected that would insure reports which would be regarded as authoritative and to be relied upon, inasmuch as the basis for them would be direct information from those actively engaged in railway operation.

The writer became the head of the Commission, the membership as constituted consisting of Lieutenant George Wood Logan, of the United States Navy; Lieutenant Hugh T. Reed, of the United States Army; Clement F. Street, Mechanical Engineer; William H. Jackson, Photographer; Edward Everett Winchell, Artist; and Harry F. Stevenson, Stenographer.

The Field Columbian Museum issued credentials, to wit:

"To Kindred Institutions, Railway and Transportation Companies, Officials and Individuals:

"The Baltimore and Ohio Railroad Company's exhibit of the Evolution and Development of the World's Rail Way at the World's Columbian Exposition, together with the exhibit of the Pennsylvania Railroad Company, as also of the New York Central and Hudson River Railroad Company, the Chicago and North Western Railway Company, and the Illinois Central Railroad Company, now constitute in the Field Columbian Museum of Chicago the Museum of the World's Rail Way, of which Mr. J. G. Pangborn is Honorary Director.

"Mr. Pangborn, who conceived, constructed, collected and perfected the Baltimore and Ohio Exhibit, and was the Company's Exposition Executive, is, under the authority and as a representative of the Field Columbian Museum, visiting the various countries of the world for the purpose of securing historical and other material, originals, models, drawings, photographs and representations of divers characters, illustrative of the progress and development of the railway in all lands, that the Museum of the World's Rail Way shall be rendered complete to date in its divisions of Permanent Way, Structures, Motive Power, Equipment, Operation, Management and Literature.

"Co-operation in the labors to this end will be heartily appreciated and fittingly acknowledged by the Field Columbian Museum. In bespeaking the kindly interest of kindred institutions as well as of railroad and transportation companies, officials and individuals, in the efforts of Mr. Pangborn and his associates, it is in the full be-

Canadian Pacific
1893

lief that the outcome will be a Museum of the World's Rail Way in every respect worthy of recognition throughout all climes, and adequately typifying the greatest single interest in the world, whether viewed from the standpoint of influence upon progress or financial importance.

"Through the President and Secretary, with seal affixed, this thirteenth day of August, eighteen hundred and ninety-four.

"THE FIELD COLUMBIAN MUSEUM.

Signed, "EDWARD E. AYER,
"*President.*

:SEAL:

Signed, "MARTIN A. RYERSON,
"*Vice-President and Acting-Secretary.*"

The Secretary of State of the United States granted letter as herewith:

"DEPARTMENT OF STATE,
"WASHINGTON, August 2, 1894.

"To the Diplomatic and Consular Officers of the United States:

"GENTLEMEN:—It affords me much pleasure to herewith introduce Mr. J. G. Pangborn, who is about to commence a tour of the world in the interest of the Museum of the World's Rail Way, which is a component part of the Field Columbian Museum of Chicago.

"I cordially commend Mr. J. G. Pangborn, Honorary Director of the Museum of the World's Rail Way, and his associates, to your official courtesies, and ask for them such assistance as you may be able to render in the furtherance of their investigations.

"I am, gentlemen,
"Your obedient servant,
Signed, "W. Q. GRESHAM."

These credentials were supplemented by letters of introduction and indorsement from President Haines of the American Railway Association, President Depew of the New York Central and Hudson River Railroad Company, President Roberts of the Pennsylvania Railroad Company, President Van Horne of the Canadian Pacific Railroad Company, President Fish of the Illinois Central Railroad Company, President Higinbotham of the World's Columbian Exposition, Director-General Davis, and Chief Smith of the Department of Transportation Exhibits.

Compound Wooten 1893

The itinerary decided upon after a general consideration of distances to be traversed, and climatic conditions to be regarded, was to make London the initiative point, the metropolis of the world being the headquarters of railroad companies in almost every land. Thence to Morocco via rail to Marseilles and steamer to Tangier, commencing there to work eastward on the northern coast of Africa, taking in Algeria and Tunisia. Then by steamer to Jerusalem, the Syrian Coast, Port Said, the Suez Canal, Egypt and the Nile. Again by steamer southward through the Red Sea, and via Aden and the Indian Ocean to Ceylon. Thence passing to India, and by rail to Madras, Bombay, Kuwachee, the northwestern border, Baluchistan, Afghanistan, Kashmir, Lahore, Delhi, Agra, Darjeeling, Calcutta, and in fact all the leading centers of the great continent. Steamer to Rangoon, the capital of Burmah, passing over the railway line to Mandalay, the capital of Upper Burmah. Returning to steamer again, proceed to Penang and Singapore. From the latter named point to Bangkok, the capital of Siam, and thence to Batavia in Java, and on via New Guinea, Thursday Island, etc., to Brisbane, the capital of Queensland. A month or thereabouts in Australia, a week or more in New Zealand, and then from Adelaide via King George's Sound and Western Australia to Hong Kong, Canton, Shanghai, Pekin and other Chinese ports and cities. Next to Corea and on to Japan. Remain a month, and then cross the Sea of Japan, enter Russia at Vladivostock, the terminus of the Trans-Siberian Railway. Proceed inland over it and by steamers on the navigable rivers and the post-roads reach Samarkand, the terminus of the Trans-Caspian Railway, passing on to the Caspian and the Black seas, and to Rehst. There taking caravan to Teheran, the capital of Persia, and after a few days' stay, by caravan again to Bagdad, and down the river Euphrates to the Persian Gulf, the Arabian Sea, and out into the Indian Ocean. By it direct to Zanzibar, and thence down the eastern coast of Africa via Mozambique, Orange Free State, Madagascar, Zambezia, Delagoa Bay and Natal to Cape Colony, thence up the west coast via French Congo State, Liberia, Senegambia, Madeira and Cenna. Debarking and proceeding inland in Morocco to Fez, the capital, Morocco City, etc., to Tangier. Crossing thence to Gibraltar, the work on the continent of Europe beginning with Spain. In succession Portugal, France, Italy, Greece, Turkey, Austria, Switzerland, Germany,

the Netherlands, Russia, Finland, Denmark, Sweden, Norway, and returning to England to complete the labors in the United Kingdom. Then by steamer to Buenos Ayres, and six months devoted to South and Central Americas, the West Indies, Cuba, Haiti, Mexico, and thence home.

The tour will require two and a half years' time to complete, and the progress will have to be steadily maintained to do it within the period named. The Commission is at this writing in Russia, the initial year of its travel having been marked by the most cordial reception everywhere, and an interest in its labors so widespread and deep as to constitute the strongest incentive to the greatest possible effort. The co-operation proffered is most general, extending as a matter of fact to the leading governments of the world.

The Commission carries letters of introduction and commendation from Her Majesty's Secretary for Foreign Affairs to the officers administering the governments of all the English Colonies and Possessions, and in addition special instructions were issued to the Government of India relative to the facilities to be extended and attention shown. Like letters have also been issued by His Majesty's Secretary for Foreign Affairs of Germany, by the Secretary of Foreign Affairs of France, by His Majesty's Secretary for Foreign Affairs of Austria, by His Majesty's Secretary of State for Foreign Affairs of Portugal, by His Majesty's Secretary of State for Foreign Affairs of Italy, by His Majesty's Secretary of State for Foreign Affairs of Spain, by his Majesty's Secretary for Foreign Affairs of The Netherlands. His Imperial Majesty's Secretary of State of Russia has issued special instructions relative to the journey of the Commission through Siberia and Turkestan, which provides for English-speaking representatives of the Government being in attendance in order to facilitate progress and afford every opportunity for investigation and study.

The outcome as a whole of the work of the Commission cannot be other than of the largest importance, inasmuch as not only will the history of the past be established in all material respects, but the facts as to present progress and practice be authoritatively secured, systematically recorded, and eventually so reported upon as to enable comparison in all details of operation and conduct, affording a study and comprehension of results reached upon the various systems of the world which must prove of the greatest practical worth.

164

"Director General"
B&O. 1893

THE date, 1894, upon the title-page, was anticipatory of issuance that year, and the sheet was so passed through the press. In reality, the time of issue is the summer of 1896. Those versed in book-making will readily appreciate the situation in the preparation and completion of a work of this character. Others, it is hoped, will like-wise regard the consummation as commensurate. A potent influence in the deferrence was the author's isolation from all mail intercourse with the outer world for a period of nearly six months, when the incompleted portions of the Trans-Siberian Railway in Asiatic Russia were being traversed in sledge, and the investigation and study of the plans, surveys and general purposes of this great Governmental undertaking, so kindly authorized by the Imperial Authorities, were being pursued. Final proofs, matters in connection with the completion of the index and other concluding details, were thus unavoidably delayed. However, the subject-matter, practically wholly historical, is in no wise affected, and the work is the bet-ter for the additional time given to its perfection. This is true as to the mechanical as it is to the letter-press

Index to Contents

LOCOMOTIVES

LOCOMOTIVE DESIGNERS AND BUILDERS

CARS

CAR BUILDERS AND DESIGNERS

STEAM CARRIAGES

STEAM CARRIAGE BUILDERS AND DESIGNERS

PERMANENT WAY

RAILWAYS

RAILWAYS—Continued

MISCELLANEOUS

Index to Illustrations

MOTIVE POWER

MOTIVE POWER—Continued

PERMANENT WAY

PORTRAITS

MISCELLANEOUS